CATHERINE
HARRIS

trotman

Media

UNCOVERED

2ND EDITION

Media Uncovered

This second edition published in 2007 by Trotman
an imprint of Crimson Publishing
Westminster House, Kew Road, Richmond TW9 2ND
www.crimsonpublishing.co.uk

© Trotman 2004, 2007

First edition published 2004 by Trotman and Co Ltd
Reprinted 2006

Author Catherine Harris; second edition updates by Dee Pilgrim

Designed by XAB

British Library Cataloguing in Publication Data
A catalogue record for this book is available from the British
Library

ISBN 978 1 84455 139 2

Typeset by Mac Style, Nafferton, East Yorkshire
Printed and bound by Creative Print & Design, Wales

CONTENTS

ABOUT THE AUTHOR   VII

ACKNOWLEDGEMENTS   VII

CHAPTER 1
WHY READ THIS BOOK?   1

CHAPTER 2
WORKING IN THE MEDIA   3

CHAPTER 3
JOBS IN TV   9

CHAPTER 4
JOBS IN FILM   30

CHAPTER 5
JOBS IN RADIO   45

CHAPTER 6
JOBS IN NEWSPAPERS AND
MAGAZINES   53

CHAPTER 7
JOBS IN BOOKS AND
JOURNALS   65

CHAPTER 8
JOBS IN NEW MEDIA   79

CHAPTER 9
GETTING IN AND GETTING ON   90

CHAPTER 10
FURTHER INFORMATION   104

About the author

Catherine Harris is a freelance journalist. She has written for national newspapers, including the *Guardian*, the *Evening Standard* and the *Sunday Mirror*. She has also worked as a researcher in TV and radio at the BBC and in independent production companies.

Acknowledgements

Researching this book was great fun as I met so many wonderful people. Thanks so much to all those who agreed to be interviewed about their glorious media careers. Thanks also to everyone at Trotman for all their help.

CHAPTER 1

Why read this book?

This book offers an overview of working in the media. It will give you an idea of what media jobs entail so you can start thinking about whether a job in the media is for you. We've given you lots of leads to follow up. This book is a fantastic place to start research into your future. If you find the right industry and the right job for you, the reward will be a fulfilling, satisfying and enjoyable career. Who knows, you might actually look forward to the alarm going off in the morning!

This book is packed with real-life case studies. We've gone undercover and spoken to people working in loads of different media jobs in the UK. They've told us the truth – warts and all – about what it's like to do their job. They also offer advice about how to get in and get on in their area.

The media is a broad term covering a range of different sectors, different jobs and different products. But there is one thing that all jobs in the media have in common: they are highly competitive. To get in and get on you have to have talent, determination and the ability to make the most of every situation. Each one of our case studies says successful media careers are made on long hours. But most say it's worth it, because they love the job.

THE POWER OF THE MEDIA

As an example of how all-encompassing and powerful the media is, take Boots the Chemist's face cream No 7 Protect and Perfect serum. This own brand product costing less than £20 languished on the shelves of Boots unnoticed until March 2007, when a BBC programme in the *Horizon* series entitled 'Professor Regan's Beauty Parlour' was transmitted. In it Professor Regan discussed the fact this product may actually help reverse the signs of ageing. Although the product wasn't mentioned by name, within hours people all over the country were talking about it. *The Times Online* chatroom and other news websites were abuzz with comments about it, it was being mentioned on radio, and within days the BBC lunchtime news had footage of customers queuing to get their hands on a bottle of this precious serum. The consequence of all this media fuss was that the following weekend 160,000 bottles of Protect and Perfect were sold around the country and even though Boots' factory upped production to 20,000 bottles a week it still couldn't keep up with demand.

It is difficult to get into the media. If, having done your research, you still want to work in the media – go for it. During the research for this book I spoke to a successful BBC TV news reporter. She told me that after university she applied to one of the most prestigious MA courses in the country for broadcast journalism. Not only did she not get a place, her interviewers told her she should think of a different career – they didn't think she'd make it as a journalist. If she'd listened to them she would have given up before she'd started. Instead, she applied for a different course, secured a place and went from strength to strength, eventually landing a plum job in broadcasting. What's the moral of the story? Don't be put off too easily. Hard work and focus can help you overcome obstacles and achieve your goals. Always listen to advice, but the only person who can decide whether you would suit a particular career is you.

CHAPTER 2

Working in the media

A CHANGING MEDIA LANDSCAPE

It's an exciting time to start a career in the media. Innovations like wireless technology and broadband are changing the media environment. From book publishing to radio and newspapers, all media sectors are embracing new technologies as a means of communicating and interacting with their viewers, readers and listeners.

The possibility of transmitting DVD-quality video over broadband is having a significant impact on the broadcasting landscape. Already this year the BBC has launched its first 'on demand' internet service called the iPlayer. The player is free and allows viewers to download up to 400 hours of BBC programmes a week so they can watch their favourites exactly when they want to. The programmes can be chosen via an on-screen guide and once downloaded are stored for 30 days before deleting themselves. By the end of 2007 this service should be available via YouTube and eventually the BBC hopes to deliver the service via cable and mobile phones. (If you'd like to access the iPlayer go to www.bbc.co.uk/iPlayer.)

In May 2007, magazine publisher EMAP launched *Heatworld.com* a state-of-the art website based on its award-winning magazine *Heat*. The website has already proved more successful than its print version.

The merger of Telewest with Virgin Mobile has resulted in Virgin Media, which offers customers a total TV, broadband and phone package, including on demand films, TV and music videos.

And with Sony and Microsoft investing in online gaming – allowing players to compete over broadband networks – it's easy to see the massive impact of broadband on all media sectors.

Convergence is the buzz-word of the media's near future. One possibility is that TV, as we know it, will become a thing of the past. The new home appliance will be a media centre, something between a TV and a PC. It will be able to play and store music, videos and photos and will have a built-in personal video recorder. In fact, Microsoft has already launched a product that does all these things.

The government is backing technological change in the media all the way. According to some, the digital revolution isn't coming – it's already here. A government target has been set to have 100% digital TV usage in the UK by 2010. According to the 2007 Ofcom annual report, in September 2006, 73% of households watched digital television on their main set. Some media commentators say the digital revolution is being over-hyped and that the government will have to reconsider the feasibility of a total digital switchover by 2012. But already DSG International (formerly Dixon's) has announced it will stop selling analogue television sets by the end of 2007. The point is: the future of the media is being carved out now. No one knows for sure exactly what the future holds. You could be part of that future.

DOG EAT DOG

Skillset is the Sector Skills Council for the media and according to its 2006 census 205,550 people are employed across the industry (although it estimates that with people employed in related industries the figure is closer to 500,000), with interactive media (web, internet, online gaming, interactive TV, mobile content) being the biggest sector (48,600). When you think how hugely influential the media is, this figure is actually quite small (by comparison, the construction industry employs over 2.41 million people) and so competition for jobs is extremely fierce. You can increase your chances by doing your research well and building up experience for a specific part of the media.

In general, the more creative a job is, the more sought-after it is. New entrants often overlook jobs in the business and finance sides of media sectors. This is a mistake. If you are numerate, have strong organisational skills and are good at detailed work, these positions offer increased stability, and sometimes offer greater longevity. Other job areas may be less secure. Do bear in mind that the creative side of the industry is dominated by young graduates (apparently 62% are under 35 years old, while less than 10% are over 50 years old). Apart from being a good route into the media, a financial media background can be useful in attaining a senior management position. This is true in publishing and new media too.

If you're starting out in media you should look at the opportunities presented by the changing technological media environment. In times of rapid change, becoming an expert in a new area can give you a career advantage. Practical skills relating to new technologies will stand you in good stead to capitalise on opportunities offered by the changing environment. For example, the 'new media' section of *Work Guardian* is dominated by website jobs such as web co-ordinator, web communications officer, web assistant and web assistant editor.

FREELANCE OR FULL TIME

Once you do get in you can work either as a freelance – being your own boss and moving from contract to contract – or as a staffer – working full time for a single organisation. Freelance work can leave you financially high and dry: there's no holiday pay, and when your contract finishes you have to find new work, fast. However, rates are generally good because of the insecurity, and freelance work does allow people more flexibility. In theory freelancers should be able to take months off when they need to, rather than being fixed to holiday terms decided by an organisation. Read the case studies in this book – from a mixture of freelancers and staffers – and decide which you would prefer.

AREAS OF THE MEDIA

In this book we've divided the media up into the following areas:

- TV

- film

- radio

- newspapers and magazines

- books and journals

- new media.

The possibilities for a new career are endless, with each area offering far-reaching opportunities. You may dream of being a presenter on Radio 4 or a DJ on a music station. Or you may want to work in academic publishing as opposed to children's or blockbuster romantic fiction. Whatever your interests, you can pursue them in a media career.

As each area is discussed in more detail later on, you will see there are opportunities for crossover. A standard career path for a broadcast news journalist, for example, often encompasses both radio and TV reporting; and local newspaper reporting is a good route into online news writing.

New technologies in broadcasting are likely to shift the traditional definitions in the media sector even further. Being flexible and adaptable has always been part of working in the media. Read up as much as you can about the wider media context.
Understanding the changing relationships in the converging media landscape could help you on your way to an exciting and varied career.

WHO THE BIGWIGS ARE - TOP JOBS IN MEDIA

According to the *Guardian*, these are the ten people who are considered to have the most powerful jobs in the British media:

1. Chief Executive, Google – Eric Schmidt
2. Chairman and Chief Executive, News Corporation – Rupert Murdoch
3. Director General, BBC – Mark Thompson
4. Executive Chairman, ITV – Michael Grade
5. Chief Executive, BskyB – James Murdoch
6. Founder, Virgin and Virgin Media – Richard Branson
7. Co-founder and Chief Executive, Apple – Steve Jobs
8. Chief Executive, Ofcom – Ed Richards
9. Controller, BBC2 and 6Music, Controller, BBC Popular Music – Lesley Douglas
10. Editor, *Daily Mail*, Editor-in-Chief, Associated Newspapers – Paul Dacre

Source: *Guardian* Media 100, 2007

All these people have excelled in the media environment and come out on top. To find out more information, like how much they earn and what age they are, go to the fantastic *Media Guardian* website, www.guardian.co.uk – the mother of all media websites!

Many of those on the bigwigs list once started with the simple idea that working in the media might be for them. For some inspiration, do some research into their careers and find out how they got to where they are today. You never know, in a few years' time, it could be you.

THE COMMISSION FOR RACIAL EQUALITY'S RACE IN THE MEDIA AWARDS

People from ethnic minorities are under-represented in the media. BECTU, the largest broadcasting union, has in the past called TV 'institutionally racist', and Greg Dyke, the former BBC

Director General, once described the BBC as 'hideously white'. According to Skillset's employment census in 2006, only 7.4% of the media workforce is from ethnic minorities (although this is a slight increase from 2004).

Launched back in 1992 the Race in the Media Awards are the annual awards of the Commission for Racial Equality (CRE) and recognise outstanding achievements by the media in their treatment of issues relating to race relations and integration. Nominees come from all areas of the media and are recognised because they have helped to challenge negative stereotypes about the many different communities that make up Britain. After a hiatus of two years the awards were re-launched in 2005.

RACE IN THE MEDIA AWARD WINNERS 2006

- Media Personality of the Year: Sir Trevor McDonald

- Media Organisation: BBC

- Broadcast Soap: Silver Street (BBC Asian Network)

- Factual Television: Tonight With Trevor McDonald (ITV1)

- Television News: BBC London News

- Feature Film: *Kidulthood* (Revolver)

- National Newspaper: *Guardian*

- Local Newspaper: *Peterborough Evening Telegraph*

- Radio News: BBC Radio Five Live

- Specialist Magazine: *The Nursing Standard*

Source: www.cre.gov.uk/rima2006

CHAPTER 3

Jobs in TV

TV QUIZ

Here's a quick quiz to give you an idea of some of the skills needed to work in TV.

1) You're a runner in an independent production company. You've worked a nine-hour day and are on your way home, but the development producer asks you to look through some casting tapes for a new presenter for a programme aimed at 16–24-year-olds – she thinks that you will be able to give a youth angle.

   a) You're tired so you tell the producer you are going home but are happy to look at them tomorrow.
   b) You say you can't help as you don't know anything about casting.
   c) You'd love to help as you watch a lot of TV and have got loads of ideas about what makes a good presenter.

2) You're a researcher on a three-part documentary about dating. Shooting starts tomorrow. It's 6pm and one of the couples you've confirmed has had an argument and no longer wants to take part in the programme. You've got to find a replacement and fast.

a) You work with the team and call everyone you know to try and find a new couple. When that doesn't work, you go out on the street and ask random people. Eventually you persuade the best friend of the couple who dropped out to take part, but not until midnight that night!

b) You collapse under the stress, start crying and go out and get drunk.

c) You leave it up to the assistant producer – after all, he gets paid more money.

3) **You've been promoted from a runner to a position buying transmission rights for the music and archive footage on a current production. You are in charge of the budget and have to convert dollars to pounds sterling. You have to stay late most nights to deal with companies in Los Angeles.**

a) You leave at 6.30pm on the dot. They can't expect you to stay any later on what they're paying you.

b) Figures have never been your strong point and you mess up, overspending massively on the budget.

c) You work efficiently. You stay late, but not every night, and your budget comes in bang on target.

ANSWERS

1) The correct answer is (c). You're a runner, so it will be expected that you are dying to get on. It may be late, but the producer is asking you to help and giving you an opportunity to learn. Runners who get promoted not only demonstrate that they can work hard, they must also show they are genuinely interested in the industry.

2) The correct answer is (a). Working in TV, you will constantly be in situations in which you have to troubleshoot, and quickly. Lots of things can go wrong so everyone on the team has to be able to come up with quick solutions to problems.

3) The correct answer is (c). Being able to handle a budget is an important part of many jobs in production. The flexibility to stay late is also an important part of working on productions.

TV OVERVIEW

Of all media careers, jobs in TV are probably the most sought after – look at these numbers.

FASCINATING FACT

Broadcast television employs 25,000 people, 16% of the overall audio visual industries' workforce. The overall total for television has been relatively stable for several years. Of those 25,000, 16% are freelance, 49% of them women and 8.3% from ethnic minorities. Permanent jobs are the norm, with freelancers making up 27% of the workforce.

Source: Skillset

IT'S A RATINGS GAME

Ratings are hugely important in TV. While the BBC can afford to be slightly less ratings-driven than commercial channels, most TV shows are required to get a big audience fast or they are likely to be dumped or shelved to a less popular time slot. Imagine that happening to something you'd sweated blood and guts over. Ratings are measured by the Broadcasters' Audience Research Board (BARB), an organisation that knows the viewing habits of 11,500 people in 5,100 homes.

Worldwide spin-offs are also becoming increasingly important. The British are the second largest TV exporters in the world. With formats like *Strictly Come Dancing* and *The Weakest Link* selling around the world, British shows make up around 13% of the global TV exports market. But that's nothing compared to American TV exports, which account for 68% of global TV imports. The success of shows like *Lost, Desperate Housewives* and *24* has been phenomenal. The final episode of *The Sopranos* was an international news story.

WHERE THE JOBS ARE

It will probably not surprise you to learn most jobs in TV are
located in London and the South East, but this does not
necessarily mean you will have to move to the capital to work in
the TV sector. Below are the numbers (and percentage
breakdown) of who works where geographically. Do bear in mind
these figures also include Scotland, Wales and Northern Ireland
and are inflated by the many freelancers who work in both
terrestrial and independent TV – basically hopping between jobs
as they come up. Many of the regional broadcasters, such as
Granada, have extremely good reputations. In fact, in 2007 the
UK's first TV production apprenticeship (The Advanced
Apprenticeship in Media Production) was offered exclusively to 20,
16–22-year-olds in the North West, where business is booming.
The initiative is backed by Granada and the BBC, which is
planning to move five of its existing London departments to the
new Salford MediaCity:UK (see below).

TERRESTRIAL TV EMPLOYMENT BY REGION/NATION

Northern Ireland	627	3%
Scotland	1,346	6%
Wales	1,157	6%
All London	*1,1587*	*56%*
South East England	792	4%
South West England	1,081	5%
East Midlands	466	2%
West Midlands	520	2%
East England	397	2%

FASCINATING FACT

MediaCity:UK is the BBC's new creative hub at Salford, Greater Manchester, where it plans to relocate five major departments to create a new national centre for media manufacturing. It will bring together the BBC, other major broadcasters and the independent sector on one purpose built site with state of the art production facilities for design, programming, advertising, video games, music and cinematography across the digital media industry. Skillset North will be closely involved with Mediacity:UK, helping to train the next generation of highly skilled media professionals. (For more information, check out the nations and regions section at www.skillset.org.)

Yorkshire & the Humber	1,068	5%
North East England	328	2%
North West England	1,450	7%
Total	**20,817**	

INDEPENDENT PRODUCTION EMPLOYMENT BY REGION/NATION

Northern Ireland	612	3%
Scotland	1,173	6%
Wales	1,166	6%
All London	*1,1661*	*56%*
South East England	1,479	7%
South West England	669	3%
East Midlands	43	
West Midlands	450	2%
East England	475	2%
Yorkshire & the Humber	713	3%
North East England	148	1%
North West England	2,383	11%
Total	**20,972**	

The major UK TV players are listed below.

- Anglia
- BBC
- Border TV
- Channel 4
- Discovery Channels
- ITN
- ITV
- ITV Granada
- ITV Wales
- London Weekend Television (LWT)
- Meridian
- S4C
- Scottish Television

TOP TIP

Have a look at www.bbc.co.uk/jobs/ for a fantastic overview of the opportunities available if you work for the UK's public service broadcaster. Go to Channel 4's *4Talent* site at www.channel4.com to find out more about its new talent schemes to help young people get on in the industry.

REAL LIVES – THE FREELANCE LIVE DIRECTOR/PRODUCER ON KIDS' TV

Graham Gordon, 28, London

The job

My job is coming up with ideas to fill the airtime and working with an associate producer, director and a runner to make scintillating, captivating live TV. Things can go wrong when you're live and that's the buzz. Anything can happen. You can make the best TV or the worst TV. In theory if you rehearse well enough nothing should go wrong but that doesn't always happen in practice. When it goes well it's a fast and fun job. Live TV is like juggling on a motorbike!

Best bit

The buzz, putting an idea into practice and putting it out live, it's happening there and then so it's reactive and interactive. Usually there is a fun bunch of people working in kids' TV, everyone's up for a laugh. Most people working in live production are in their 20s and early 30s – except the technical people, who tend to be more a mix of ages. Live production is quite draining, so I think inevitably people move on after a bit. It's a young person's game in the sense that it's exhausting. A lot of people go into management in their 40s.

Worst bit

Security in TV – there's very little when you're freelance. Most people worry about that. But the upside of job insecurity is that people give their all. So everyone is pushing themselves and doing the best they can. That makes for a very creative environment. The other downside of TV is there are some arrogant and pretentious people around. But you get used to that.

Career path

Once I'd got in as a runner it was just a question of making contacts and developing my skills. I didn't do any courses. I just learnt on the job and started picking up digital video skills as soon as possible – that's key to getting on. I took any work I could get but I always knew I wanted to direct and that's what I aimed for. I moved from company to company getting as much experience as possible on each job.

CAREER LADDER

Freelance Live Kids' TV director/producer
↑
Disney Channel producer/director
↑
Director for Paramount and Trouble
↑
Researcher, AP independent production company specialising in kids' TV
↑
Researcher, Children's Channel
↑
Head Runner, at Nickelodeon
↑
Runner, facilities house in Soho
↑
Assistant, Thresher's wine merchants
↑
English at university

Runner, otherwise known as general dogsbody. Entry-level job in the industry: so-called because it entails so much running around!

JOBS IN TV

CREATORS AND PRODUCTION

This involves coming up with ideas for programmes, developing ideas, putting those ideas into practice and making them happen. From *Who Wants to be a Millionaire?* to *EastEnders*, TV shows are made through the blood, sweat and tears of a team of people turning a creative idea into TV reality. For most of these roles digital video (DV) skills are increasingly useful.

This area includes roles such as:

- **Producer** – puts a programme and team together. The job requires creativity and organisation and the ability to handle budgets. In some strands, such as documentaries, the producer may also be the director.

- **Director** – uses his or her creative vision to shape the look and often content of a programme. In charge of the set and filming. In drama, the director is the big cheese.

- **Scriptwriter** – writes scripts on existing soaps, dramas or comedies or creates an original script for a new programme or series.

- **Assistant producer** – works with the producer and director to generate ideas and make the programme happen. In documentaries, this role will often involve securing case studies and probably some filming.

- **Presenter** – the face of a programme. Needs to perform well consistently, often under pressure.

- **Researcher** – one rung down from the assistant producer. Has ideas, finds case studies if necessary and researches programme content. Can be helpful to know how to use a DV camera.

- **Production assistant** – an assistant to the production department, a mainly administrative role but a good place to learn from.

SKILLED TECHNICAL AND ARTISTIC PEOPLE

TV is a technical business. Nothing would happen without a skilled team of technical experts to facilitate the director and producer's vision and transmit the programme. Even better, there are some technical areas with skills gaps, where well-trained people are always needed. These include production accountants, broadcast and electrical engineers and carpenters.

Includes roles such as:

- **Floor manager/assistant director** – manages the studio from the floor. On location this role is called an assistant director.

- **Lighting camera operator** – sets up and operates the camera in studio and on location.

- **Camera supervisor** – co-ordinates a team of lighting camera operators.

- **Editor** – cuts footage together with the director/producer. An editor needs to be both highly technical, visual and a perfectionist.

- **Sound technician** – uses equipment such as a boom. Sound technicians are responsible for a programme's sound.

- **Broadcast engineer** – designs, maintains and operates broadcast equipment.

- **Production designer, art director, set designer** – are responsible for the design and creation of the set.

BUSINESS, LEGAL AND FINANCE

TV is a business. Someone's got to see the big picture and count the money! Without the business and finance people, the TV industry would collapse.

These areas include roles such as:

- **Rights assistant** – deals with contracts, release forms (legal forms signed by contributors to permit broadcasters to transmit their content) and other legal administration, including rights issues relating to archive footage.

- **Media law expert and contract expert** – all broadcasters and many larger independent production companies have their own in-house lawyers to deal with everything from presenter contracts to worldwide transmission rights.

● **Production accountant** – handles the budget on production, ensuring budget is not under- or overspent.

● **Press officer** – works for a broadcaster or an independent production company, publicises new shows and maintains the company's profile and reputation.

BROADCAST JOURNALISTS

They tell the news. This is a fast-paced job, and the quality of news stories rests on the team's ability to research, interview and communicate the news.

● **Editor** – responsible for the overall news programme, makes editorial decisions and decides the news agenda and structure of the programme.

● **Producer** – works on individual stories within a news programme, either with or without a correspondent, depending on the needs of the story.

● **Presenter** – presents news programmes, often live, including interviews. Experience and broadcast skills are a must.

● **Correspondent** – a specialist news reporter, an expert in his/her journalistic area, researches stories and broadcasts TV reports, sometimes live. Experience and broadcast skills essential.

CASH

According to the most recent Skillset figures (for 2005) across the board, television professionals work on average 44.6 hours a week earning a mean annual salary of £32,239. This compares to a national average of 33.8 hours and £24,300 for the UK workforce as a whole. However, the survey also shows that the majority of television industries are based in London and the South East. Here, people in TV work longer hours and have higher salaries with the average working week being 44.9 hours and the average salary being £33,867.

Interestingly enough 32% of those in broadcast TV interviewed said they had undertaken unpaid work in order to get on in the industry, and this figure rises to 50% for those who work in independent production, showing that in the long run it really does pay to 'show willing' and do some work experience.

- **Broadcast TV** – the mean for those working in broadcast TV is £32,902, however 4% of those surveyed earned less than £12,000, while the biggest percentage (45%) earned between £30,000 and £49,999.

- **Cable and satellite TV** – here the mean was slightly lower at £32,681.

- **Independent TV** – the mean for those working for 'indies' was £32,779.

Of course, most earnings increase with age and on average 16–24-year-olds were earning just £17,372, while those over 50 years old were on £36,446.

SOME SALARY EXAMPLES
What you earn will depend on your training, experience, and who you actually work for but here are a few examples of salaries across the television sector.

TV runner	£10,000–£20,000
TV researcher	£8,000 (trainee)–£30,000
Sound technician	£15,000–£30,000
Production assistant	£15,250–£30,150
Studio floor manager	£16,000–£35,000
Camera operator	£15,000–£40,000
Broadcast journalist	£10,000–£45,000
SFX technician	£20,000–£50,000
TV editor	£20,000–£60,000
TV producer	£70,000 upwards
TV director	£200,000 upwards

TOP TIP

For more in-depth info on TV jobs and the industry, try the following websites:

www.broadcastnow.co.uk
www.film-tv.co.uk
www.productbase.co.uk
www.startintv.com

REAL LIVES - THE NEWS CORRESPONDENT

A 33-year-old BBC TV correspondent, London

The job
My job combines a mixture of researching interesting stories, writing, going out and filming and talking to extraordinary people about what they've done. Being a TV news reporter is a sociable job. We work in teams. I film with a camera crew and work with an editor. I also like working under pressure. I enjoy the discipline of deadlines. The deadline forces you to write accurately, quickly and hopefully entertainingly in the time slot you are allocated to deliver the story.

Best bit
I'm constantly trying to improve my broadcast techniques and developing how I tell a story and how I use pictures. It never gets boring.

Worst bit
It's most difficult when there isn't a story there and you're asked by an editor to make a story out of nothing. The easiest pieces are strong stories. Often I will have to battle with an editor when I don't think the story is strong enough. However, if the editor thinks it's a story, you've got to do it and it can be a real struggle finding something to say.

Career path
After university I did a postgrad diploma in broadcast journalism at the London College of Printing [now the London College of

Communication] and then I went into local radio in London – News Direct – and worked as a reporter. I spent a couple of years there and then I moved to IRN and worked as a reporter on national radio. After two years I made the move to TV reporting and reported on the ITV news channel. While I was there I did ITV breakfast news and lunchtime news. After about a year I went freelance and worked as a TV news reporter for ITN and BBC London. I then took a short-term contract at the BBC doing national news reports and subsequently was offered a staff position. Now I'm one of the BBC's specialist news correspondents.

CAREER LADDER

BBC staff TV news reporter
↑
Freelance TV news reporter
↑
News reporter, independent national TV
↑
News reporter, independent national radio
↑
News reporter, independent local radio
↑
Broadcast Journalism MA
↑
French at university

JARGON BUSTER

Rushes – **uncut film that needs to be edited so it can be shaped into the programme.**

REAL LIVES – THE CAMERA ASSISTANT

Mark Sayers, 26

When I was 12 years old I saw a camera crew outside Westminster and announced to my family 'that's what I want to

do!' At college I studied Design and Technology, and Computing and then went to Sunderland University to do a BA in Media Production (TV and Radio), specialising in TV. I got a 2:1 but I also got lots of 'hands on' experience.

The job
Now, I travel the length and the breadth of the country, staying in hotels with a load of mates having a laugh as I work on a whole variety of different shows. One day I can be on stage running around with a cameraman shooting the latest TV talent contest [Mark has recently been working on *Dancing on Ice*], then the next I'm at a football ground rigging for the biggest match of the season. I love that flexibility of working whenever and wherever I want. I'd hate to be tied to a certain number of days holiday allowance a year.

Worst bit
The uncertainty of work is definitely one of the downsides of the job because there are times when the work stops coming in, that's why I want to gain more qualifications. I have already taken a course in Steadicam [Steadicam is a specialised hand-held camera] and that helps me find work as a Steadicam assistant. My aim for my career is to become one of the top Steadicam operators in the country, to be someone people recommend for jobs, who is known for his skill and delivers it confidently every time. I want to be on stage shooting the biggest bands, or out on location working on top music videos.

What you need to succeed
In order to do what I do, I think you need to be hardworking, patient, confident, reliable, trustworthy and fit! My best piece of advice for people who want to work in TV, whether it is with cameras or anything else, is to approach companies and businesses rather than to immediately go freelance. This is because you need to learn your trade with the protection and guidance a company can offer because out in the freelance world you can't afford to make mistakes.

TOP TIP

Want to see a TV show being recorded? Get tickets from www.beonscreen.com.

REAL LIVES – THE POST-PRODUCTION RUNNER

Brendan Stuart, 24, originally from Lancaster

The job

I've been a runner in a Soho facilities house for six months. The money's terrible and it's hard work, but it's fun and I've never been so fit in all my life. Most of the work that comes through here is a mixture of TV, adverts and music videos. So it's a good learning place for me. I'm staying with my brother and the rent is cheap, otherwise I don't know if I could manage on what I earn. The company I work for is quite small, so they've only got about six edit suites. I've got to pick up tapes around Soho and drop them off, all on foot. I often walk about five miles a day. My job also entails going and picking up coffees and making toast for the clients and getting them whatever they want from the outside world.

Best bit

A more senior runner here has already started learning to edit and is allowed to use one of the empty suites in her free time. The other runners are fun and all about my age. We have a real good laugh about everything.

Worst bit

Edit suites are dark, airless places. That can feel a bit depressing in the summer. The hours are really long. If I'm doing the late shift I've got to wait until the last client goes, which can be anything up to midnight and beyond. It is tough and if you didn't want to get on you wouldn't do it. It's basically like going back to school and starting in your first year. I need to laugh; otherwise I could feel like a servant. There are fun creative people in TV and music videos and there are idiots. That means that some people do treat you badly – asking you to warm up their cappuccinos and that kind of thing.

CAREER LADDER

Runner, editing facility in Soho

American studies at university

Of the UK's 1,100 or so independent television production
companies around 700 are based in London
                                    Source: www.creativelondon.org.uk

REAL LIVES - THE TV NEWS PRESENTER

Louise Minchin, Presenter, News 24

The job
I present three and a half hours of live evening news in which I
usually do numerous live interviews on the main news stories of
the day. To do my job you've got to be a perfectionist, inquisitive,
quick on the uptake and not panic under pressure. I'm the sort of
person who loved exams!

Best bit
I love the fact that it's live and fast moving. At News 24 we're
always trying to be first with the news and first with our
interviews. It's exciting to be part of that.

Worst bit
I'm the last line of defence, so if something goes wrong I've got to
deal with it live on air. It drives me nuts when news stories have
been written wrong.

Career path
I started out on work experience at the BBC World Service in
1992. I rang up and organised a placement after university. That
meant working free for six weeks, making the tea and getting
some hands-on experience. After that I graduated to a paid job as
a production assistant for the *Today* programme. I then left the
BBC to do a postgraduate course in radio at the London College
of Printing [now the London College of Communication]. I'd
recommend that to anyone – it was excellent. Then I got a job as
a reporter on Radio Berkshire.

After two years I moved to News Direct where I worked as a presenter and reporter. Then I got my break into TV reading the news bulletins at Channel Five [now five tv]. My next move was to my current presenting job at the BBC. There's been a lot of hard work involved in my career but I've also had the odd lucky break too. I was actually interviewing for a reporter's job at the BBC when they asked me if I could do some presenting on BBC News 24.

CAREER LADDER

Presenter, BBC News 24

↑

Presenter, Channel Five news

↑

Presenter and reporter, News Direct

↑

Reporter, local radio

↑

Postgraduate radio journalism course, London College of Printing

↑

Production assistant, *Today* programme

↑

Work experience as production assistant, BBC World Service

↑

University degree

LOOK AT ME! I WANT TO BE A PRESENTER!

Most of us who've watched Ant and Dec as they tease celebrities in the jungle or mess around in front of camera on Saturday nights for enormous amounts of money have thought, 'I'd love to do that!' Ant and Dec, two of the most popular presenters on TV today, do make it look easy. Budding presenters beware – it's really not. While presenters like Ant and Dec chat to the camera they've got people talking in their ears, they have to take cues and look at the right camera. And often they have to work live. That's why anyone who wants to be a presenter has got to be good under pressure. Getting your first shot at presenting is difficult.

But those that make it do so with a mixture of persistence, luck, hard work and being the right face at the right time.

Presenters like Ant and Dec who work in light entertainment often come from a performing background, while news presenters (see Louise Minchin's case study on page 25) come from a journalistic background.

Working in production can be a good starting point. Daisy Donovan was picked from the production team of the *11 O'clock Show* to front the cult comedy programme.

THE LIGHT ENTERTAINMENT PRESENTER
Here's the story of a 20-something presenter who was working as a researcher.

'I was working as a researcher in light entertainment documentaries in Anglia TV in Norwich. We were looking for a presenter for a series about buying a house abroad. We couldn't find the right one so I begged them to let me have a go. I did an audition and got the job. It was just being in the right place at the right time. It is also about having the right face. I think I look better on camera than off it!'

JARGON BUSTER

Call sheet – **information for a shoot, including the shot list and contact details of everyone taking part. Created by someone in the production team.**

REAL LIVES – THE BROADCAST GRAPHIC DESIGNER

Jane Aspinwall, 31, London

Any fan of Graham Norton's TV series, *The Graham Norton Show*, will have seen Jane's work as she is responsible for the title sequences and for all the graphics generated throughout the show. Jane and four friends have just set up a new company called Timeslice Films, which specialises in arc cameras capable of capturing 360 degree shots – a technique developed on the *Matrix* trilogy of films – and they are hoping to do more film work as well as work on TV shows.

The job
For Graham's talk show on the BBC I have two days preparing with the writers and the production staff giving them the graphics they require. Then on Wednesday I take the graphics and my machinery to the studio where I set it all up, check the feeds and make sure everything is working. Then I am in charge of everything that is on screen from videotape (VT) clips to audience-point-of-view takes (PVTs). I also do some editing and then after the show I have to dismantle all the equipment. I work in quite an unusual way because I own my equipment – most people don't and have to hire it in. Although I have done a coding course in order to learn HTML, apart from that I am self-taught. I've learned on the job because the software changes so quickly you are always having to learn new systems. However, what you do need to have is a very good grounding in design and a thirst for knowledge.

Best bit
I quite like the pressure and the buzz in the studio because it is so fast paced. Also I just love anything to do with design and designing and the creativity of producing beautiful images. I'm also unusual in that I like the technical side of being in charge of setting up the machines.

Worst bit
It is high pressure and with any studio work you always get a lot of shouting. So, if you're a person who likes quiet and calm and working methodically I'd say this end of the business is not for you, you'd probably do better in post-production where there aren't 5,000 things going on at once. To work in the studio you need to be very quick, be able to make decisions and definitely have very good technical knowledge. Also, the hours are very long and quite weird because it is so labour intensive.

CAREER LADDER

Setting up her own company, Timeslice Films

↑

Freelance contract as motion graphic designer for Graham Norton's BBC show

↑

Freelance contract as motion graphic designer for Graham Norton's Channel 4 show

↑

Freelance concept design for TV pilots

↑

Shadowing people at Sky TV (basically work experience)

↑

BA Honours in Textile and Print Design

RELATED OCCUPATIONS

- Advertising

- Film

- Marketing

- Multimedia

- Performing

- Print journalism

- Public relations

- Radio journalism.

CHAPTER 4

Jobs in film

FILM QUIZ

Here's a quick quiz to give you an idea of some of the skills needed to work in film.

1) **You're a camera operator, it's late at night and you're still filming. You wish you could get something to eat.**

   a) You start thinking about food and drift off so you mess up the shot.
   b) You shout 'Cut' and tell everyone you need food now.
   c) You concentrate and put all your energy into the filming. You love film and want to make sure you get the perfect shot.

2) **You're a first assistant director. Some bit-part actors are getting rowdy and disturbing the director who is thinking about the next scene.**

   a) You go over and tell them in no uncertain terms to shut up.
   b) You go pink and whisper, 'Can you be quiet, please?'
   c) You figure they will quieten down in a minute.

3) You're an editor on a film with a huge budget. You've spent
    hours editing and re-editing the same scene.

    a) You hate detail. Overall it looks OK. You call it a night.
    b) You are a perfectionist bordering on an obsessive. You
        don't even notice what time it is, you just want to get this
        section of the film looking perfect.
    c) One of the actors/actresses came in earlier to look at
        some rushes – you got his/her phone number and all you
        can think about is your forthcoming date.

ANSWERS

1) The correct answer is (c). Being a camera operator requires a
    massive amount of concentration. You've got to be agile,
    technically minded and creative.

2) The correct answer is (a). First assistant directors need to
    keep discipline on set and have to make sure everything goes
    as smoothly as possible for the director. This job requires
    strategic thinking as well. You have to be able to see
    problems before they happen and take steps to overcome
    them.

3) The correct answer is (b) Editors have to be extremely visual
    and also technically adept. An essential part of the job is
    attention to detail. An editor works closely with the director to
    produce the final film and should be a perfectionist with the
    ability to focus on tiny sections of the film as well as having a
    good overall picture of the director's vision.

FASCINATING FACT

**Eyes down on set. It is said that some famous actors insert
an 'eyes down' clause into their contract. That means that
when you pass the actor on set you have to look down. So
when you do finally make it on set – no staring! No
rubbernecking either!**

FILM IN NUMBERS

Although it is very difficult to accurately judge the number of people who work in film (many people who are freelance constantly swap between working in film and TV depending on what jobs are available) according to Skillset's *A Bigger Future: The UK Film Skills Strategy*, approximately 34,000 people work in the film industry in this country. Many of the people who do work in film tend to be older than those who work in TV and the industry is still predominantly male, despite the best efforts of the industry itself to address this issue. Another very salient point is up to three quarters of those employed in the film sector have periods of unemployment within any given year. However, that doesn't seem to stop people from wanting to get into films and now is a good time to do so. Film is a growing industry. In 2003 the worldwide film industry was worth £42.3 billion and it is growing by 6.3% a year. In 2007 it is forecast that consumers will spend £54 billion watching films in the cinema and at home. British film technicians have a worldwide reputation for excellence and British-backed films, such as *Notes on a Scandal* and *Pride and Prejudice*, or the huge Hollywood productions that are shot here, such as the James Bond and Harry Potter series, showcase those talents.

JARGON BUSTER

Facilities house – a hub of technical know-how. This is where the editing happens, where the sequence, colour, sound and special effects are born, creating the film from the raw material of the rushes. Editors are crucial to the final product. Some directors edit themselves, while others will oversee the editing process carefully.

FILM ROLES

CREATORS AND PRODUCTION

These people come up with ideas for a film, develop ideas, put ideas into practice and make them happen.

Some roles are listed below.

- **Producer** – develops the original idea, buys the rights, commissions the scriptwriter, finds the director, hires the crew, manages post-production and lots more. Film producing is a complex creative and managerial job, and the producer has responsibility for the film's ultimate profitability.

- **Director** – uses his or her creative vision to shoot the film; works closely with the producer. This is a highly creative job, and the director must lead a team of creative and technical people to carry out his or her vision.

- **Scriptwriter** – writes and rewrites the film script according to the producer's and director's wishes. Will either be working on his or her idea or be commissioned to fulfil a brief. Likely to have an agent.

- **Production assistant** – helps organise film production, from booking transport to and from set, to producing the daily call sheet. An administrative role.

SKILLED TECHNICAL AND ARTISTIC PEOPLE

Each film is a huge technical undertaking. Working on set will often mean being on location and working flat out. Without the technical and artistic part of the crew the film just wouldn't happen.

Roles include:

- **Director of photography** – uses his/her technical knowledge of lighting and film to create the look the director desires.

- **Costume designer** – dreams up and makes costumes for the actors following a brief.

- **Editor** – cuts the rushes to make the final film. This is a highly significant role. The editor will work closely with the director to shape the film. Some directors come from an editing background.

- **Production designer** – working closely with the costume designers and director of photography, the production designer is head of the art department. He or she works to co-ordinate the film's overall look and ensures it comes in on budget.

- **Clapper loader** – assists camera operators, including loading and unloading film, looking after the camera equipment and working the clapperboard.

BUSINESS AND FINANCE

Film is a multi-million dollar business and there are plenty of jobs related to finance, publicity and distribution.

Roles include:

- **Production accountant** – manages the film's budget and controls the spend during production. Must be organised, good with figures and good under pressure.

- **Film PR** – promoting the film during the cinema and DVD/video release dates.

ENTRY-LEVEL JOBS

There are a few ways into film. You could be like Quentin Tarantino and write an amazing script that gets picked up; or become a hugely bankable star like Robert Redford and then move into directing. Or, much more realistically, you can work your way up from the bottom.

We've all got to start somewhere. Think Martin Scorsese, Steven Spielberg, Pedro Almodóvar, Jane Campion – inspiring names. But I bet at one time or other in their careers they've made the tea and worked themselves silly for little money or thanks. Film is a highly technical business, and useful technical skills will always help you progress up the career ladder. Whatever you start out as, keep your eyes and ears open. Remember, you need to learn everything you can to get on. Listen to advice and be keen. However, you are a human being. Be diplomatic but don't let anyone push you too far.

Entry-level jobs include:

- runner

- wardrobe assistant

- production assistant

- make-up/hair assistant

- clapper loader/camera assistant

- props assistant

- sound assistant

- post-production runner/assistant editor

- lighting assistant

- casting assistant

- third assistant director

- assistant location manager

- art department assistant.

THE ART OF THE SHORT FILM

With the rise of affordable, good-quality digital cameras has come the rise in importance of the short film format. These days anyone studying film, be they a director, camera operator or even make-up artist, can really get on by working on a short film. In a way it acts like a visual CV showing people exactly what you are capable of. Here's what Pippa Rimmer of innovative promotion and distribution shorts company Futureshorts says:

'No one is going to ask you to make a feature film when you are a runner, although that is one way into the industry. But I would say to anyone out there who wants to get into film, just go and make your own work. Get as much practice in as you can and shorts are perfect for doing that because you can do a string of shorts in the time it would take you to do a feature.

'The boundaries with digital are endless because it is so much cheaper to use (than film stock). The cost of using film is just so prohibitive. You can also get cheap programmes that come with computer software to edit films further reducing the cost. The upshot is anyone can become a filmmaker these days – not everyone can become a good filmmaker – but anyone can have a go and I think that's great.'

There are now countless short film festivals where you can get your work seen and these can lead on to much greater things. For instance, director Andrea Arnold won an Oscar for her short *Wasp* and then went on to make her first feature, *Red Road*, which won the jury prize at the Cannes Film Festival. First Light Movies funds the making of short films by young people aged between 5 and 18 years old. Find out if you could get funding at www.firstlightmovies.com. For more information on the shorts format visit Futureshorts' website at www.futureshorts.com.

FASCINATING FACT

Two thirds of the UK's full-time film industry jobs are in London and 75% of all UK post-production facilities.
Source: www.creativelondon.org.uk

CASH

Like TV, film can be an incredibly lucrative business, but not usually when you're starting out. Most runners and other entry-level jobs are paid at extremely low rates. Start developing a taste for tuna sandwiches.

The following are the minimum weekly rates agreed in the Freelance Production Agreement 2006, as agreed by BECTU, the largest broadcasters union and PACT, the Producer's Alliance for Cinema and Television (figures courtesy of the BECTU website www.bectu.org.uk).

	40-hour week	72-hour week
Art department assistant, technical assistant	£282	£620
Production secretary, third assistant director	£315	£693
Clapper loader, junior make-up/ hair assistant, publicity assistant	£420	£925
Sound assistant, graphic artist, assistant script supervisor	£435	£958
Wardrobe assistant, props person, assistant editor	£481	£1,059
Dubbing editor, production co-ordinator, third assistant director	£510	£1,122
Boom operator, location manager, focus puller, grip	£556	£1,223
Production buyer, set decorator, unit publicist	£591	£1,301
Camera operator, art director	£638	£1,404
Editor, production accountant, construction manager, costume	£721	£1,587

CUTTING EDGE
See as many new films as possible – not just at the cinema. The Sheffield International Documentary Film Festival is where all the aficionados can be seen checking out the latest talent in documentary film making and factual TV (www.sidf.co.uk).

REAL LIVES – THE PRODUCTION ASSISTANT

Kate Cheswick, 22, Leeds

The job

I assist the production co-ordinator and the producer during the pre-production stage and filming. My role is mainly straightforward administration. I deal with phone calls, queries, produce daily call sheets and assist the production co-ordinator in booking cars to get all the people to the right places. I also make sure everyone's got the right version of the script. I'm involved in booking sparks (electricians) and I liaise with the agencies that hold information about all the freelance contributors to a film. These agencies are called diary services and hold the diaries of everyone from freelance technicians to freelance people in the art department. You can ring up and ask for a particular person and they'll tell you if they're free on the day you want them. They will also recommend people for specific jobs.

It's a great place to be if you want to become a producer or part of the production team that puts together a movie. I work closely with the production co-ordinator and producer. It's also a good position from which to learn about all the different people on film and what jobs they do. It's one step up from being a production runner. If you want to be a director you'd be better off trying to get a job as a floor runner. As a production assistant I hardly ever make it to the floor to see the filming taking place. However, floor runners are hard jobs to get – production assistant jobs are probably easier. To be a production assistant, you need good computer and organisational skills and bags of enthusiasm. It is low pay. I have been paid as little as £50 a day. I'm usually on a daily or weekly rate. If the production office is on location, you go wherever filming is taking place.

Best bit

Everybody comes into the production office so you meet everyone. Films are quite gossipy and in the production office you get to hear about everything that's happening. It's really interesting seeing how the budget works and it's satisfying seeing all the organising you've done coming together – like when all the people you've booked turn up.

Worst bit
The job is totally dependent on your relationship with the production co-ordinator and the producer. If they're big shouters it can be quite hard. Hours are long and when you're working it's likely to be seven days a week. Like a runner, the production assistant is the first into work in the morning and the last to go at night. Also, even though you're no longer a runner, you may get asked to do a runner's job like get the sandwiches and coffees. Basically you're bottom of the pile. In my case I was lucky. I formed a good relationship with a production co-ordinator. As soon as she became a producer she took me with her as a production assistant on her next jobs.

Career path
I studied English at Leeds University. While I was there I volunteered at film schools in Leeds and worked on student productions for free. After university I got a job in a TV drama as a runner, then became a runner on a film and then a production assistant on a film.

CAREER LADDER

Production assistant on film
↑
Runner on film
↑
Runner on TV drama
↑
Runner on student films
↑
English at university

TOP TIP

Read *Screen International* for the latest in news from the film world. Go to www.screendaily.com.

REAL LIVES – THE FREELANCE ART DIRECTOR

Mark Harris, 46

I started my career as a runner for a producer at Pinewood Studios and my duties included making tea, running errands, having prints made from draughtsmen's drawings, and assisting with the construction of study models. I then worked my way up the ladder from junior draughtsman to art director. All these grades come under the jurisdiction of the Association of Cinematograph Television and Allied Technicians (ACTT) and the lines of demarcation are very rigid.

The job
I'm responsible for the environment in which the artists perform the script, whether it's a built interior (a studio, say) or a dressed location. I set the scene and work in partnership with the director of photography in creating the mood and I am responsible to the producer for controlling the cost. I love being part of a creative team that builds a fantasy from the printed words in the pages of a script. However, my work is constantly at the mercy of several outside forces: the exchange rate, interest rates, and government tax breaks all contribute to the tidal movements of the business. You can never predict from one year to the next whether the business is going to be busy or quiet and so I'm currently looking for opportunities that might take me into something a little more stable. My entire career has been a learning process and over time I've developed passions for certain aspects of design and architecture. I'm currently teaching myself a number of different computer programs that will be useful to me in the areas of drawing and pre-visualisation and I think it's important to move with the times and technology.

What you need to succeed
You need to be flexible to survive in the film industry; there isn't another rollercoaster ride like it. You also need to learn to accept rejection. It's nothing personal but people often look for different qualities when they are building a team and you might not fit their criteria for the sake of the tiniest nuance. Finally, always be punctual. People who consistently show up late may think they can get away with it, but it never goes unnoticed.

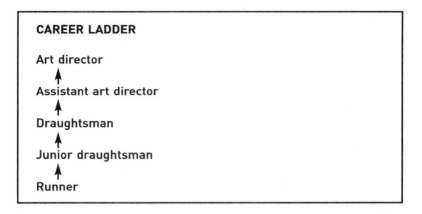

CAREER LADDER

Art director

Assistant art director

Draughtsman

Junior draughtsman

Runner

REAL LIVES - THE ASSISTANT CASTING DIRECTOR

Gillian Edmunds, 26, London

The job
The job is choosing the right actors and actresses for specific productions in film and TV. I assisted an independent casting director. People came to us to find actors for big productions. As an assistant casting director my job was to constantly look out for new actors.

To work in casting you need to know all the faces out there – not just Julia Roberts! You've got to be imaginative and have a good eye for faces. You've got to constantly spot new talent. That means you have to be pretty dedicated, looking out for bit-part actors with some flair and going to student productions and end-of-year shows.

Forging good relationships with key agents is also important. Agents can be very difficult. For example, sometimes they will tell you that their client can't read a script that you want them to read for. That's a way of hyping the actor to make them look really busy.

You've got to have good people skills and be polite and courteous. It's not for the faint-hearted. Actors come in and tell you their life story and it feels awful when they are rejected for the job. In the end, with the amount of auditions you see, most actors are rejected. I just found that really depressing so I decided it wasn't for me.

FASCINATING FACT

The UK has a stunning film history and a massive film archive to prove it. The National Film and Television Archive is run by the BFI and is situated in Berkhamstead, Hertfordshire. It currently contains 50,000 fiction films, 100,000 non-fiction titles and over 625,000 TV programmes. The BFI says it needs £34 million in order to build new storage facilities for this priceless national treasure and also to digitise old prints. Digitising just one 90 minute film from an original colour negative can cost £8,000.

REAL LIVES - KEY GRIP

Keith Manning, 38

The job
Grips are essentially responsible for the mounting and movement in shot of the camera and are responsible for the safety of the rest of the camera team. This involves using various pieces of equipment – from simple mounts to dollies with track and cranes. The complicated equipment carries a huge responsibility for its operation and the safety of the crew and the public around you. I'd like to push my career forwards and so am considering getting a license to drive scissor lifts and cherrypickers. I may also get my professional underwater qualifications.

Best bit
I love the variety of places I work, both in Britain and internationally, and it is great to have the power to choose which job I'm going to take and how much holiday I'm going to have in a year.

Worst bit
There is always the insecurity of never knowing when the next job is coming in. It also means you can't make plans for the evenings as you are never sure when you will finish work and there are long periods spent away from home.

Best piece of advice
I would always say join the recognised grips training scheme run by FT2. This is what I did and I have a NVQ level 3 in Camera/Grip.

REAL LIVES – COMPOSER FEATURE FILMS

Guy Farley, 44

The job
I not only compose the themes for feature films, but I also arrange, orchestrate and produce electronic demos for each piece I write. I also produce the final musical product and conduct the orchestra or players during recording sessions. Finally, I oversee the mix and deliver the finished music to the producers. I manage the job every step of the way including all aspects of music utilised in the score. I book the players, programmers, studios and engineers from start to delivery.

Best bit
The feeling of having written something good and new. The moments I stand before the orchestra and the first rehearsal are great, and working with talented performers is an honour. Receiving communications from people I don't know who have been affected by my work is the other end of my being affected by a piece of music composed by someone else!

Qualities needed
You need tolerance, patience, perseverance and above all belief in oneself. Sometimes you find yourself working under extreme

pressure and you have to have the ability to deal with that and with difficult people, particularly those with egos and insecurities. You need the foresight to accept yourself as part of the process in a production and so must not be self-centred or egotistical. Being creative can bring on a gamut of human emotions from ecstasy to rage and it is important to find a balance. Ultimately, I would love to be recognised for my work, in that I would like my scores and music to be well received and enjoyed. Of course, I would be elated to receive a nomination for an award, or even better, an actual award for my music!

RELATED OCCUPATIONS

- Advertising

- Marketing

- Multimedia

- Performing

- Print journalism

- Public relations

- Radio journalism

- TV.

CHAPTER 5

Jobs in radio

RADIO QUIZ

Here's a quick quiz to give you an idea of some of the skills needed to work in radio.

1) **After sending off loads of CVs, you get offered low-paid work experience on local radio. You've done a week and it's been tough going.**

   a) You decide to pack it in. You're being underpaid anyway.
   b) You go into work and make a huge fuss that you want to be treated like someone special – after all, you're giving up your free time.
   c) You keep going back and focus on what you can learn from the experience.

2) **You're the studio manager on a live breakfast show. You are responsible for the output of the programme. A technical hitch means you've played a jingle at the wrong time.**

   a) You keep calm, sort it out and go on to the next thing.
   b) You run out of the studio in shame.
   c) You hate pressure and wish you had a different job.

3) A meeting is called to come up with ideas for a new celebrity slot on the national music radio station at which you're a production assistant.

   a) You just want to be told what to do so you can get on with it. You try and get out of the meeting.
   b) This is your big chance – you can't wait to shine in the meeting. You've got so many ideas you don't know which ones to share.
   c) You've got masses of administration to do and you just feel bogged down so you can't be bothered to waste your time.

ANSWERS

1) The correct answer is (c). To get on in radio you've got to be persistent – you can't give up at the first hurdle. Work experience depends very much on who you're working for. You could be assigned to making the tea for days on end. But you have to get the best out of it. Be polite, enthusiastic and interested in radio. Make the tea but also ask radio-related questions. Ask if you can help out in any other way. You have to be diplomatic. You can always learn something from any situation. Remember, everyone there will probably have done low-paid bottom-rung work – they won't want to hear you whingeing about it.

2) The correct answer is (a). The studio manager has to be able to keep calm under pressure and foresee and correct any problems. He or she also has to keep an ear out for any possible legal problems – interviewees may say something slanderous, for example.

3) The correct answer is (b). Most non-technical roles in radio require you to be an ideas person. Good broadcasting thrives on constant creativity. It's a fun part of the job. Ideas and writing skills are seen as essentials for non-technical jobs in radio.

JARGON BUSTER

RCS Master Control – most of the radio industry has now gone digital and uses hard disk play-out systems like RCS Master Control. Go to www.rcsworks.com to find out more.

RADIO OVERVIEW

According to Radio Joint Audience Research (RAJAR), which compiles radio audience figures, in the first quarter of 2007, 45 million people over the age of 15 listened in at some time. That's 90% of the population. Of those, 58% listened via digitally enabled radio (DAB), this figure being up 43% year on year. There are currently over 350 individual stations in the UK so there are plenty of opportunities for employment out there. (For more information on audience breakdown visit the RAJAR website at www.rajar.co.uk.)

Radio can be broken down into the following categories:

● music

● news

● sport

● talk

● drama

● magazine programmes.

FASCINATING FACT

Over half of all TV and radio employees work in London, representing a workforce in excess of 25,000
Source: www.creativelondon.org.uk

CREATORS AND PRODUCTION

This includes jobs such as:

● **Presenter** – researches stories, does interviews and sometimes 'drives' the desk (i.e. is responsible for sound output, including jingles and music). Presenters of news programmes are likely to come from a journalistic background.

- **Radio production assistant** – this is a great place to start to find out about the industry. The role is basically administrative. You could be doing anything from typing up scripts to answering the phone or checking details to responding to listeners' letters and emails. This role is hands on and in the thick of things.

- **Broadcast assistant** – in this role you can start learning broadcast and technical skills. Administrative tasks are involved but you are also likely to be involved in research and production.

- **Producer** – a role for a creative and organised person. The producer comes up with programme ideas, handles the budget and oversees production.

TECHNICAL

This area includes jobs such as **technical operator/studio producer**, who makes the sound output possible. In live radio a studio operator manages all the technical aspects of radio transmissions. When radio is not live but pre-recorded this person records, edits and mixes the audio.

JARGON BUSTER

Sound editing packages – **these are used to edit sound in the studios. You can get these packages for your computer and turn it into a recording studio. Adobe Audition and Pro Tools are both commonly used in the workplace. Packages can be downloaded for free on the internet.**

CASH

As with other media jobs, starting salaries are not particularly high. According to the Prospects graduate recruitment website (www.prospects.ac.uk) you can expect to be paid the following in these radio production jobs. Popular presenters, like Chris Moyles or Christian O'Connell, competing on a high-profile breakfast slots command considerably higher fees!

- **Broadcast assistant** – £15,000–£23,000 a year in London. Outside of London rates will be lower at around £13,000–£19,000. At senior level (after ten years experience) rates are between £17,000–£25,000.

- **Radio producer** – starting level is around £10,000–£12,000, while senior level will be £30,000–£80,000 a year. Freelance producers should expect to get between £150 and £300 per day.

JARGON BUSTER

Mixing desk – **produces the sound output and includes faders and monitors.**

REAL LIVES – THE RADIO DJ

Bali Deol, 21, originally from Huddersfield, is a presenter on Awaz FM 107.2 Community Radio, Glasgow

The job
I present my own show at drive-time and do an R&B top ten. Presenting isn't just about talking! It also includes lots of research. I've got to interview people on the show so a lot of background work goes into that. I've just finished my degree in media, theory and production at Paisley University. It included a mix of theory and practical stuff. We did everything from advertising to radio production and journalism. I also considered doing the media course at Caledonian but I chose the Paisley course because it was more hands on. I'm glad I did, as I really enjoyed it and I've found the practical skills I learned useful in this job.

Best bit
I feel passionate about broadcasting. I've always wanted to work in radio and TV. My show is a mixture of R&B, bhangra and hip

hop. It's music I love and the job allows me to be how I am. I'm quite an extrovert and presenting is a perfect job for that.

Worst bit
The research can get boring because it's demanding.

Career path
While I was at university a friend of mine was doing a show on Awaz on Friday night. He asked me if I wanted to do it with him. It worked really well and we had a lot of fun and the show had energy and was popular. After that I got a joint presenting slot on drive-time and then I got my own show.

CAREER LADDER

Presenter on community radio

↑

Co-presenter on community radio

↑

Media, theory and production at Paisley University

TOP TIP

Go to the Radio Academy website at www.radioacademy.org/gettingin where they have a fantastic guide to getting into radio with tips from the great and the good in the industry.

JARGON BUSTER

***Driving a desk* means the same as operating the mixing desk in the radio studio.**

For more information go to www.prospects.ac.uk, www.bbc.co.uk, Channel 4's site www.channel4.com or the Skillset site at www.skillset.org

REAL LIVES – THE RADIO FILM CRITIC

James King, Radio 1

The job

It's kind of scary but I've never wanted to do anything other than what I am doing now. My careers advisor said I should be a librarian, but I ignored him! I did all languages at A-level (English, German and French) and that led me to a film and literature course at university, which in turn led me to a Postgraduate Diploma in Broadcast Journalism. Finally, I took a MA in Film Studies. From there I went straight into working for Radio 1.

Now I review all the new films and DVDs each week and try to help listeners with their film questions like 'was that Richard Branson doing a cameo in *Casino Royale*?' Yes it was, by the way. Behind the scenes I am also involved in Radio 1 film promotions, deciding which film guests should come on, and sorting out competitions.

Best bit

As a film critic you have to have patience and an open mind, although watching bad Martin Lawrence films at 9am press screenings puts both of those things severely to the test. But I love watching films, pure and simple.

What next?

The day my desire for the escapism of film goes, it's all over. Before that happens I'd like to do more writing because having something in print that lasts longer than a five-minute radio slot is something I aspire to. Also, I'd like to complete the film PhD I started and very quickly gave up on, if I ever get the time.

What you need to succeed?

For anyone out there who would like to do what I do I'd say watch lots and lots of films. Background knowledge is essential to make you stand out from being just another person with an opinion. Also, it is crucial to remember that for most people, going to the cinema is just another thing they occasionally do at the weekends. Films are not the be all and end all.

RELATED OCCUPATIONS

- Advertising

- Film

- Marketing

- Multimedia

- Performing

- Print journalism

- Public relations

- TV journalism.

CHAPTER 6

Jobs in newspapers and magazines

NEWSPAPERS AND MAGAZINES QUIZ

Here's a quick quiz to give you an idea of some of the skills needed to work in newspapers and magazines.

1) You are offered a junior writer's job on a current affairs magazine.

   a) Great! You're a news junkie. You read papers, watch news and keep up to date with world affairs – this is your dream job.
   b) Kofi who?
   c) Yawn – I always switch over when the news is on.

2) You're a journalist working in a press agency specialising in financial journalism. Your editor doesn't like your story. She gives it back to you, tells you in no uncertain terms what she thinks of it and screams you've got to rewrite your 600 words in half an hour. You're on a deadline for a national newspaper – the features desks need your story now.

a) You say 'I can't do it' and burst into tears.
b) You ask the editor to be specific about what extras and changes she wants and knuckle down and do it.
c) You say it's a boring story and you can't be bothered to rewrite it, get your coat and go home.

3) **You're doing a feature on a big soap star for a women's magazine. The soap star is also going to be on the cover. When you arrive to interview her she is incredibly rude to you.**

a) You say, 'Stuff your interview – I'm not being spoken to like that'.
b) You punch her in the face and walk out.
c) You are diplomatic and try to win her over. There's no way you're leaving without your story and that's that.

ANSWERS

1) The correct answer is of course (a). There are magazines about everything. Use your interests to help you get on. Gravitate towards what fascinates you. This will not only help you to enjoy your job but will also help you to be good at it.

2) The correct answer is (b). There will be times in newspaper journalism when you are so stressed you think you will explode. But you have to make deadlines and give the editor what he or she wants. You can't be too touchy if your work is criticised.

3) The correct answer is (c). You're not the star, you're the journalist. You've got to get your story. Diplomacy is a large part of the job. Someone at the magazine, if not you, will have worked hard to secure a big interview and no one will accept you coming back without a complete interview.

JARGON BUSTER

Copy. **The journalist's text is referred to as copy, as in 'Hurry up with that copy! The features desk needs it now!'**

JOBS IN NEWSPAPERS AND MAGAZINES

EDITORIAL AND DESIGN

Writers, editors and designers work together to create stimulating, attention-grabbing and accurate content for newspapers and magazines. Once content has been researched and written, it must be checked, altered if necessary to make it adhere to a consistent 'house style' and made to fit the page. Many newspapers and magazines have now branched out into other media and include an interactive online site.

Jobs in this area include:

- **Editor** – edits final content, decides on the overall content and ultimately takes responsibility for those decisions. For instance, the editor of *The Times*, Robert Thomson, was responsible in 2004 for overseeing the paper's introduction of a new compact edition (rather than its traditional broadsheet format), a move that saw sales figures rise but is said to have cost its owner (Rupert Murdoch of News International) approximately £45 million. Editorships are highly coveted, especially those of well-known titles such as *The Times*, so job vacancies do not come up often.

- **Sub-editor** – checks and rewrites copy written by journalists before it's laid out on the page. All copy must be put into 'house style' by the sub and checked for potential legal problems. In some cases the sub-editor will also design and lay out the pages.

- **Magazine journalist** – generates and researches ideas, carries out interviews and writes copy. On smaller magazines writers may be involved in many other parts of the magazine process including sub-editing and layout.

- **Newspaper journalist** – reports the news and writes features on everything from current affairs to fashion. Writing skills, tenacity and attention to detail are essential.

BUSINESS AND FINANCE

Newspapers and magazines are big business and profit is driven by sales and advertising revenue, aided by marketing and advertising sales (the revenue created from companies paying to advertise in the publication).

Jobs in advertising sales involve securing lucrative adverts on the pages of a publication. To succeed at this job you have to have drive and enjoy working with targets in a pressurised environment.

For more information on working in magazines and newspapers go to the Prospects website, at www.prospects.ac.uk.

For more information on working on local newspapers go to www.newspapersoc.org.uk.

TOP TIP

Magazine and newspaper journalists often become specialists in an area, anything from health to technology. This can help career advancement and helps freelancers to get work.

CASH[1]

● **A sub-editor** on a local paper or small magazine earns somewhere between £13,000 and £16,000. On a larger regional this rises to around £18,000, while those with more experience can earn £22,000 to £37,000. A chief sub-editor on a national can earn £50,000 plus.

● **A magazine journalist** just starting out is likely to be earning around £18,000 to £24,000. As his or her career progresses the money will go up to around £19,000 to £35,000 plus. Those

1. Figures from Prospects website (www.prospects.ac.uk)

working on bigger publications or who become editor-in-chief can earn between £22,000 and £63,000 plus.

- **A newspaper journalist** training on a local newspaper will earn around £17,500, while those working on a national earn around £40,000. At more senior level, depending on the size of the publication and profile of the journalist, salaries range from £50,000 to £100,000 plus. There is huge money available if you make it big!

Do bear in mind in 2006 the average salary for ALL journalists was just £22,500, so you have to be highly ambitious to earn big bucks in this trade.

TOP TIP

For a round-up of international news and the best from newspapers across the world read *The Week* **magazine. Go to www.theweek.co.uk for more information.**

REAL LIVES – THE SENIOR REPORTER ON A LOCAL NEWSPAPER

Simon Conlan, 25, Manchester

The job
Every week I do about four lead articles of 400 words, then three or four second lead articles of maybe 300 words and then eight fillers which is maybe 120 words and then five or six NIBS – news in briefs which are around 50 words. You spend a lot of time on the phone researching stories and going out and about meeting people. We work 9am–5.30pm but you tend to work a bit later most nights, and occasionally you might have a night meeting.

Best bit
I like the variety. I cover everything from crime, planning and community to transport and local politics – as long as it's on my patch. I enjoy writing. It's great to see your name in print at the

end of the week. They're a nice bunch of people at my paper and there's a culture of going out and having fun after all the hard work is done. Most people tend to be quite young – early to mid-20s. There are a few exceptions as some people come to it older. There are eight of us on my paper, six reporters, a chief and a news editor. In our office there's four different newspapers. So there's lots of opportunity to meet interesting people.

Worst bit
Pay is bad on local papers. Even in London trainees only get something like £18,000 a year. That's for a graduate with a postgraduate journalism qualification. There's also something called a death knock, which I think is the worst part of the job. Luckily I haven't had to do too many of these. A death knock is when someone from your paper's area dies in an unusual way and your editor sends you out to get a comment from their nearest relations. That's obviously horrible and no one likes doing it. Once I had to track down the mother of a murdered teenager, go to her house, and ask her for her side of the story. It can feel like you're really invading people's privacy. The job can be quite stressful. Sometimes you feel the deadlines are good as there's a bit of adrenaline going. Other times, if you've got three or four stories to write, and you're under pressure, it can feel a bit much. I'd say you have to like pressure if you want to go into news reporting. Newspapers work on pressure.

Career path
I started as a trainee reporter. I got the job after my pre-entry exams at the end of my journalism course. After 18 months as a trainee you sit your final exams and if you pass those, you're a qualified senior reporter. Now I'm thinking about what to do next. I could stay at this local paper and hope to get a chief reporter's job. If I take that route I'll take on more management functions, stop writing so much and start editing other people's work with a view to becoming an editor of my paper. The other option is to move to a trade magazine or to move to a regional daily like the *Manchester Evening News* or the *Birmingham Evening Post*. I think I might try a trade magazine as then I could become an expert in an area like health or technology and then move to a national. To get on to a national newspaper directly from a local, I would have needed to try to sell some stories while I was working here or get weekend shifts on a national newspaper. To make the

local to national leap, you've got to be hugely ambitious and not want any free time. I was having too much fun to do that!

CAREER LADDER

Senior reporter, local newspaper
↑
Trainee reporter, local newspaper
↑
Postgraduate journalism course
↑
Politics and Sociology at university

JARGON BUSTER

News – as opposed to features, which are more analytical, news has to be about something new to readers – otherwise it isn't news!

REAL LIVES – EDITOR OF *THE WEEK* MAGAZINE

Caroline Law, 32, London

The job
As editor I decide the content of the magazine and make sure all the copy is up to the finished standard. I do some of the writing myself, but also have to spend time re-writing inadequate copy and making decisions about pictures, headlines and captions. I manage the editorial team, and am responsible for making sure we keep within budgets. I spend a lot of time discussing the final content with other editorial staff – it's not an autocracy – and deciding things like the cover image. From time to time, I have meetings with the advertising team to discuss ideas for maximising revenue.

Best bit
It's an easy-going office, the work is interesting, and it's well paid. It's also nice to be in charge.

Worst bit
The long hours, and having to work at weekends. I spend hours on Saturdays and Sundays wading through the papers.

Career path
After university I went into publishing but ended up working on business books, which I found deeply boring. After two years, I was so fed up I jacked it in and took a 50% pay cut to work as an office dogsbody at *The Oldie* magazine. My title was editorial assistant. I was there for two years, during which time I was promoted to sub-editor/assistant editor. It's a small magazine so I was able to move up the ranks quickly. I then moved to *The Week* as a junior writer/assistant editor. I was made deputy editor and then became editor.

CAREER LADDER

Editor at *The Week* magazine
↑
Deputy editor at *The Week* magazine
↑
Assistant editor at *The Week* magazine
↑
Assistant editor at *The Oldie* magazine
↑
Editorial assistant at *The Oldie* magazine
↑
Business publishing
↑
Law at university

To be fully informed on up-to-the-minute news, read the BBC and *Guardian* websites every day at www.bbc.co.uk and www.guardian.co.uk.

REAL LIVES - THE NATIONAL NEWSPAPER PICTURE EDITOR

Dave White, 36, London

The job

It's divided mainly into two areas. Firstly, I commission photographers: assign them jobs and set up those jobs. You've got to be properly briefed (normally by section editors) so you know what is needed for the story and be able to pass that on to your chosen photographer. The other side of the job is researching pictures, usually with picture agencies. For example, if someone is doing an interview with Margaret Thatcher, you need to commission a new photograph of her and also find historical images relevant to the story.

Best bit

It's a very creative job and if you get a newspaper that appreciates photography, your job is as creative as the writer who is telling the story.

Worst bit

It can be a very high-pressure environment and you have to meet deadlines. If you are a person who doesn't like to work at a frenetic pace, a newspaper might not be for you. The job of picture editing in a magazine is less frenetic as you've got longer to make decisions.

Career path

I went to university and did an unrelated degree. While I was a student I did a lot of photography as a hobby. After I graduated I got an internship at Polaroid, then went to work for a photography gallery. My next move was to work on the picture desks of a fashion magazine and then a travel magazine. Finally, I moved to a national newspaper and became deputy picture editor and then eventually became picture editor.

CAREER LADDER

Picture editor, a national newspaper

↑

Deputy picture editor, a national newspaper

↑

Picture desk, a travel magazine

↑

Picture desk, a fashion magazine

↑

Assistant, photography gallery

↑

Internship, Polaroid

↑

University degree

JARGON BUSTER

The clothesline intro – so named because you can hang everything on it. A style of news reporting in which the introduction includes six questions – who, what, how, where, when and why.

REAL LIVES – THE ASSISTANT EDITOR (SHOWBIZ) OF NOW MAGAZINE

Selena Julien, 30

I've wanted to be a journalist from the age of 13. I was completely obsessed with magazines and newspapers so when I went to college I edited the newsletter there and I did my first stint of work experience with the BBC at the age of 17, when I became a runner on the *Esther Show*. It was a great opportunity as Esther was one of the biggest names on the BBC and she had a range of interesting guests on including celebrities. It was my job to look after them when they arrived, get them into make-up, and return them to the green room (hospitality) after they'd recorded the show.

The job

As the assistant editor of the busy showbiz department at *Now* magazine I have a team of seven writers and it's my job to liaise with them and decide which celebrities they will be interviewing. I organise photo shoots and negotiate fees for exclusive interviews. Each week I discuss cover ideas with the editor and I often fly abroad to do interviews. When the story broke that Jude Law had been sleeping with his nanny, I flew to her hideout in the south of France to do an exclusive interview and photo shoot with her.

Best bit

I love the variety of what I do as no two days are ever the same. There's always a buzz of excitement in the office when a big story breaks, but it is often the stories we're not allowed to report on that are the juiciest! Cracking the tougher celebrities and making them tell you their innermost secrets is every journalist's dream. Meeting celebrities is fun and travelling is also an exciting part of the job. I've flown to Miami to interview Missy Elliott and New York to interview Jon Bon Jovi and getting invites to A-list events and glamorous parties is a big plus to this job. However, once you've been to one you've been to them all and the hours can be unsociable especially when you have to work weekends. The other downside to what I do is we are constantly working under pressure to break exclusives and beat our rivals to big interviews.

The skills you need

Everyone has the misconception that jobs in the media involve flitting from one party to the next but the reality is you'll spend a lot of time doing unpaid work experience just to get your foot in the door. If you really want to work in media you need to research the job you want to do and do everything in your power to make contacts in that particular area and don't get sidelined. There's no point taking a job in marketing if you want to be a journalist. You'll just get pigeonholed and it will be virtually impossible to make the jump at a later date.

CAREER LADDER

↑

Assistant editor *Now* magazine

↑

Feature writer *Now* magazine

↑

Runner on the *Esther Show* (TV)

↑

Media and society degree at university

RELATED OCCUPATIONS

● Advertising

● Film

● Marketing

● Multimedia

● Performing

● Public relations

● Radio journalism

● TV.

CHAPTER 7

Jobs in books and journals

BOOKS AND JOURNALS QUIZ

Here's a quick quiz to give you an idea of some of the skills needed to work in books and publishing.

1) **You work in the marketing department of a book publishers. You are asked to give a presentation on anticipated sales figures for a particular series of books.**

   a) You're good with numbers so you calculate your targets and explain how you've arrived at them.
   b) You're terrified of numbers and beg one of your colleagues to do the presentation for you.
   c) You blag it and just spew some numbers off the top of your head.

2) **You're an editorial assistant. A new internet site has been set up relating to an educational book that has just been published. Your boss asks you to check through the copy for errors.**

   a) You have a quick look and miss quite a few mistakes. You're a big picture person.

    b) You have an acute eye for detail. You home in on misused possessive apostrophes like a hawk.

    c) You'd rather write the copy than read through it.

3) **You're the production director. It's your job to make sure your books and products are produced as cheaply as possible. You enter into negotiations with your paper supplier.**

    a) You're a killer negotiator. You get your company the lowest price ever for paper.

    b) You feel sorry for the paper supplier. He's always been so nice, you just don't have the heart to ask him to rethink his price.

    c) The supplier takes you out to lunch and gets you drunk – you agree to pay more for paper.

ANSWERS

1) The correct answer is of course (a). A lot of sales and marketing jobs require you to be numerate. Marketing departments have to anticipate demand correctly. If they get the numbers wrong it can be a costly mistake.

2) The correct answer is (b). Most editorial work requires you to be good at detail.

3) The correct answer is (a). As a production director you've got to be a brilliant negotiator. Production is all about producing a quality product at the lowest possible cost. It's essential that the company's bottom line is your priority.

PUBLISHING OVERVIEW

The good news is that Britain is a European publishing hotspot. We have the second largest publishing industry in Europe.

In the UK, there are approximately 4,000 book and journal publishers employing 33,000 people. The UK book and journal market is worth about £4 billion, with the top ten publishers now controlling 63% of the total market. Book publishers are centred in London with some specialist educational and academic publishers situated around Oxford and Cambridge. In Scotland, Edinburgh is the main centre.[2]

Publishing is known for its long hours and relatively low pay. But if you love books there's no greater industry to be in. Unfortunately you should forget any fantasy notions of publishing you may have in which book lovers take long lunches discussing their favourite authors. The modern publishing business is driven by financial return. Many people working in publishing will tell you the hours are long, work is stressful and costs are increasingly kept down. The financial rewards for working in publishing are not high when compared to many other graduate careers.

FASCINATING FACT

London's publishing industry has an output of £3.4 billion.
Source: www.creativelondon.org.uk

AVERAGE SALARY BY LOCATION

(The latest figures are from 2004 and should be used as a guide only)

Ireland	£28,633
Scotland	£19,389
Wales	£19,585
Central London	£24,151
Greater London	£26,000
South and South East England	£23,622
South West England	£24,345
Midlands and East Anglia	£22,563
North England	£23,550

Source: Bookcareers.com 2004. For latest figures and more information, go to Bookcareers.com

---

2. Prospects website (www.prospects.ac.uk)

According to Reuters (May, 2006), in the UK there were 206,000 books published in the year 2005–2006. This demonstrated a 28% growth from the previous year.

JOBS IN BOOKS AND JOURNALS

You could work in any of the following areas:

- general or consumer (also referred to as trade)

- children's

- educational, academic and specialist (including medical, business, etc.)

If you have a degree in a specialist area like business or nutrition this can be a good way in. Go to your local bookshop and find out who the big publisher is in your area of study. Niche publishers often prefer graduates with specific knowledge.

According to the Publishers Association, publishing functions are broken down into the following areas.

- **Editorial** – researching, writing and editing texts.

- **Design and production** – creating the look of the pages and producing the product for the printer.

- **Marketing, sales and publicity** – generating sales and calculating product demand.

- **Distribution** – supplying demand, including invoicing and stock control.

● **Rights and contracts** – dealing with authors' and publishers' rights in the national and international market.

● **Finance and administration** – dealing with finance matters including payroll and authors' royalties.

TOP TIP

Finance and accounting jobs can lead to senior management positions in publishing. Go to the Publishers Association website, www.publishers.org.uk, to find out more.

EDITORIAL

Jobs in this area are highly sought-after and this is probably the most difficult area in publishing to break into. A good entry-level job is an editorial assistant. These positions are not easy to secure. However, work experience, demonstrable passion for books and persistence can help. A publishing qualification is also useful, although not essential.

Jobs in this area include:

● **Commissioning editor** – decides what to publish. In a niche publisher, such as a careers publisher, the commissioning editor is likely to be an expert in the publishers' specialist area.

● **Reader** – assesses unsolicited manuscripts.

● **Copy-editor** – corrects errors of grammar, punctuation, spelling and meaning. A detail-focused job.

● **Editorial assistant** – assists senior editorial staff and learns basic skills related to commissioning, planning and production.

JARGON BUSTER

Slush pile – **unsolicited manuscripts sent in by authors direct to publishers. Most commissioning editors in trade publishing prefer authors who already have agents.**

DESIGN AND PRODUCTION

This includes the following jobs.

- **Head of production** – a senior management role, managing the people in the production department. He or she is ultimately responsible for keeping costs down and maintaining a financially successful and productive department.

- **Print manager** (aka print supervisor or production planner) – ensures print deadlines are met, oversees department and checks the quality of the product.

- **Production manager** – manages the production team to ensure a good quality product is delivered to the printers on time and in budget.

- **Book designer** – works to a brief to create the look of a book. This is likely to include typeface, type size and cover illustration (although the latter may be commissioned from an illustrator by the designer). Increasingly designers in publishing will also work in multimedia, including CDs and websites.

To work in production you need to be organised and numerate, as the ability to keep a tight control of scheduling and costs is essential at all levels. To be a designer you will need artistic flair and training.

CASH

The average salary by job title is as follows. The latest figures are from 2004 and should be used as a guide only.

Rights assistant	£16,196
Production assistant	£16,450
Editorial assistant	£16,648
Sales assistant	£17,667
Assistant editor	£18,945
Production editor	£19,829
Press officer	£20,556
Rights manager	£27,169
Publisher	£33,697
Editorial director	£40,592

Source: Bookcareers.com 2004. For latest figures and more information, go to Bookcareers.com

JARGON BUSTER

Backlist – no, it's not a list written on your back! A publisher's backlist is the list of their previously published books. It is an important source of revenue, because backlist sales are more predictable and dependable than frontlist (new book) sales.

REAL LIVES – THE COMMISSIONING EDITOR

Julia Moffatt, ex-commissioning editor at Scholastic Children's Books, now a freelance editor and author

The job

A commissioning editor looks for new books to publish. In my case these came from three sources. First, from our existing authors who came to me with new ideas. Second, I would come up with ideas for series; and third, agents would send in the work of authors new to Scholastic. The bit I loved was having the idea for a series and then finding the right author to fulfil the commission. Developing an idea with an author can be quite a mutual process. I commissioned the Point Crime series, for example, and that was great fun to work on. Finding the right author for an idea is a case of matching the writer's style with the concept. I once considered a famous author for the Point Crime series – obviously before she was as famous as she is now. At the time I didn't think she was right for the series, although I could see she was a wonderful writer.

Dealing with agents is another part of the job. Although some famous authors have been found in the slush pile (see above) I never found any new authors that way, so I would usually turn to agents for new authors. I would send a brief out to agents with what we were looking for. Having said that, occasionally the agents would ignore the brief and just send in whatever they wanted! And sometimes I found a great new author that way.

The final stage is when you take the finished product to the sales conference where you try to sell your list of books to hard-bitten reps. That can be nerve-wracking. I enjoy public speaking, so I always tried to make them laugh while getting the salient points across. There's definitely a bit of pain and pleasure involved in that part of the job!

Best bit
I really did love my job. Having ideas was definitely my favourite part. I used to love the energy involved in bringing an idea to fruition. It's really satisfying choosing the cover and seeing the finished work. One author I enjoyed working with was Susan Price. Her book, *The Sterkarm Handshake*, won the *Guardian* award for children's fiction in 1998 and it deserved it. It's a fantastic book, a fantasy involving time travel with a wonderful love story. She's just a brilliant author to work with. When you have a fantastic author like Susan, the job is a joy.

I also loved working on the Joslin De Lay Mysteries by Dennis Hamley. That series did an Ellis Peters type of thing – mysteries set in fourteenth-century Chaucerian times in England. Every time a new manuscript came in, it was just so exciting.

The other rewarding aspect of the job is getting letters from kids who have started reading as a result of one of your books. Being a commissioning editor for Scholastic is definitely the most fantastic job I've done.

Worst bit

When I started in the early nineties, Scholastic was a small company and a very energising place to work. As it grew it became more corporate and inevitably more political, which I didn't enjoy quite so much. Also, the hours were long. I used to start between 8:30 and 9 in the morning and arrive home at 7ish. And then I'd work on the train – so it was often a ten-hour day. Everyone in publishing works long hours. Publishing houses never have enough staff so people are always overworked.

Career path

I left Liverpool University in 1987 with an English degree. Someone suggested I do a course at the London College of Printing [now the London College of Communication] at Elephant and Castle. The course gave me a diploma in Printing and Publishing Studies, and lasted four months. It gave me a great grounding in the basics of book production, and more importantly got me my first job in publishing.

I worked in the production department at Routledge (an academic publisher) for a year, before moving into the desk editing side. I always knew I wanted to be an editor, but don't regret my time spent in production, as it taught me the basics of how a book is put together and how much it costs. As a commissioning editor, you have to make decisions about spending money or not to produce the best book you can – an understanding and knowledge of the process is, in my view, a great asset.

After another year, an opportunity arose to work for a very creative and dynamic editor. I knew that I was unlikely to get promotion where I was (I am a great believer in making the most of your opportunities – no one else will do it for you!), so I leapt at the chance to gain more of an insight into the commissioning process. After a further nine months, I realised I had hit a brick wall, and also that I wasn't sufficiently interested in academic books to stay working in that field. I saw an advert for a desk editor at Scholastic and applied for it, children's books always being a passion of mine.

I was very fortunate, not only to get that job, but to have joined the company at a very exciting time, when it was expanding and there were a lot of opportunities for promotion. In the year I joined Point Horror was launched, and I was lucky enough to get asked to expand the Point list further, by setting up the Point Crime, Romance, Fantasy and SF lists. I stayed with the company for eight years, and only left after the birth of my second child. Sadly, I think the demands of working full time in the publishing industry don't fit very well with bringing up a family, so I am now freelancing and attempting to be a writer.

CAREER LADDER

Commissioning editor at Scholastic

↑

Desk editor, Scholastic children's book publishers

↑

Editorial department, academic publishers

↑

Production assistant, academic publishers

↑

Diploma in Printing and Publishing Studies at London College of Printing

↑

English at university

TOP TIP

Look in trade journals for entry-level jobs. Try *The Bookseller*, *Publishing News* and *Print Week*. Or go to www.thebookseller.co.uk to find out more about publishing recruitment agencies.

REAL LIVES – THE PUBLICITY MANAGER, DUCKWORTH PUBLISHERS

Suzannah Rich

The job
Duckworth is an independent publisher and I am responsible for gaining coverage for our company profile, our books and our authors, and establishing excellent relationships with the press (emailing them, phone calls, letters and lunches). I arrange press campaigns for each book by targeting specific media and market titles, and I liaise with the print, broadcast, trade and online media and the authors. My job specifics include writing press releases, sending out review copies, placing adverts, arranging launch parties and signings and managing marketing budgets.

Best bit
Definitely, it is working in a non-corporate, creative environment that allows for free-thinking and resourcefulness. It is satisfying to see a book progress from the proposal stage to the finished product.

Worst bit
Publishing is very poorly paid and there is never enough money! Also the hours, in this job it is very rarely 9 to 5.

What you need to succeed
You need to be an excellent communicator, confident, outgoing, organised and structured. Also, in publishing a love of the written word is a prerequisite. As with any media, supply outweighs demand but perseverance does pay off, so do research, write to companies and if possible do work experience. People are always happy with cheap labour and once you are in at any level you can show your dedication and enthusiasm and your talents will be rewarded.

CAREER LADDER

Publicity manager, Duckworth Publishers

↑

Entry level, publicity department, Duckworth

↑

Working in a bookshop

↑

BA Honours Degree in English Literature

JARGON BUSTER

InDesign and *QuarkXpress* are desktop publishing software programs used to lay out text and pictures.

REAL LIVES – THE HEAD OF PRODUCTION, SWEET AND MAXWELL LAW PUBLISHERS

Perry Coverley, 35

The job

I head up a team of 35 people. It's a management job. I'm responsible for departmental policy and the department's overall budget. I manage overhead expenditure and the people in the department. The department produces around 2,500 products a year – these include books, CDs and online products.

Best bit

I love working with books, managing people, managing a budget and being able to make my own decisions.

Worst bit

Managing people is also the worst bit about the job. It's challenging and it can be difficult to get people to perform well all the time.

Career path

I did a print production course after university and that gave me some basic production skills. Through the course I got a job as a production assistant at Sweet and Maxwell. After a year I moved on to production controller and then I became a senior production controller and then a production manager and then head of production over about ten years.

The move from an assistant production controller up to a senior production controller is a case of being given more and more titles as your seniority increases. When I became a production manager the work became more managerial.

Go to the Publishers Association website for loads of useful information on careers in publishing and vocational courses – www.publishers.org.uk.

Have a look at www.bookcareers.com for information on latest entry-level jobs and advice and information about a career in books.

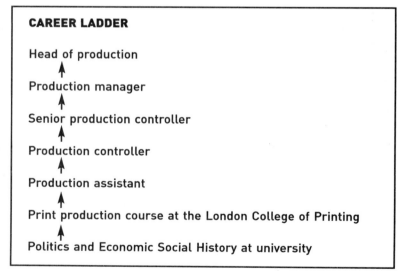

CAREER LADDER

Head of production
↑
Production manager
↑
Senior production controller
↑
Production controller
↑
Production assistant
↑
Print production course at the London College of Printing
↑
Politics and Economic Social History at university

TOP TIP

All applications to jobs in publishing should be word perfect. Attention to detail is an essential part of most publishing jobs.

WOMEN IN PUBLISHING
Women entering the industry should go to www.wipub.org.uk to find out what Women in Publishing is all about. A valuable organisation dedicated to information sharing, support and training, this site offers great advice and points out that although publishing is dominated by women, they still haven't broken the 'glass ceiling'.

RELATED OCCUPATIONS

- Arts public relations
- Bookseller
- Indexing
- Lexicography
- Library services
- Newspapers and magazines
- Translating.

CHAPTER 8

Jobs in new media

NEW MEDIA QUIZ

Here's a quick quiz to give you an idea of some of the skills needed to work in new media.

1) You're a web producer. You're in charge of setting up a new website. You've got to co-ordinate the designer, animator, coder, copywriter and a production team who are filming some video inserts to stream on the site.

   a) You're a fantastic strategic thinker. You draw up your master plan and give everyone deadlines. You're not frightened to hurry people along and keep all the suppliers on track.

   b) You're extremely creative, an ideas person, but you're a bit disorganised.

   c) You're a hard worker. You like to be a cog in a machine. Give you a task and you will complete it. But you don't want any overall responsibility.

2) You're a copywriter for the web. You have been asked to write the copy for a new health website for teenagers. You've been given some long-winded documents and asked to turn them into sparkling web copy.

a) You don't have the patience to trawl through pages and pages of writing.
b) You're interested in communicating clearly. It's worthwhile turning long complicated sentences into pithy writing for the web. That's what you love about the internet – it makes communicating so quick, succinct and immediate.
c) You'd rather get someone else to do it.

3) **You've just landed a job as an assistant in a multimedia company. You're asked to research a new bit of software.**

a) You're not interested in new technology.
b) You can't believe you're being paid to research stuff you find so fascinating.
c) Soft what?

ANSWERS

1) The correct answer is (a). A web producer has to deal with clients and negotiate costs, and is responsible for delivering the site on time and according to the brief. This is a job for an extremely organised manager who is capable of overseeing a project but who is also diplomatic and good at getting the best out of people.

2) The correct answer is (b). Writing for the web, you will be either a journalist or copywriter. With most organisations requiring a web-based customer relationship, web writers work in a range of areas. In this instance you will probably need to be a specialist health writer. The key in writing for the web is being able to structure your copy to suit a site's format. It requires the ability to write succinctly and often the ability to load the page on to the system.

3) The correct answer is of course (b). Multimedia is an ever-changing environment driven by constantly emerging technology. It helps if you are fascinated by technological change. Who knows – you may be the next person to make a mint from thinking up a new way for us to receive information.

NEW MEDIA OVERVIEW

New multi-, interactive or digital media is an exciting area to work in. It's constantly changing and includes everything from the internet and WAP phones to digital TV.

The digital revolution isn't coming – it's here already. The government wants to switch over UK television transmissions from analogue to digital signals by 2010. Already a significant proportion of the population has digital TVs. The digital revolution has increased the means and methods by which we can receive information and has shifted the viewers' place in the experience of receiving information. Now we can vote on issues on Five News, choose our favourite pop star and affect what happens on the screen. These days, viewers are part of the production team in that they create media output too.

Broadcasters are broadening their ideas about how to reach viewers. The new media division at the BBC includes *BBC Online* (Europe's largest website), interactive television and digital channels. It is thought interactive TV will lead to the largest viewing changes since colour meant people could finally understand the snooker!

It's not just TV either. The digital revolution is hitting radio too. According to Radio Joint Audio Research (RAJAR) 58% of us now listen to radio on digitally enabled sets (DAB). Listening via mobile is up 25% year on year, and in 2007 2.5 million mp3 owners listened to downloaded podcasts.

Meanwhile, online publishing is going from strength to strength. The UK Association of Online Publishers was formed in 2002, in response to the growth of the internet as a publishing medium. It now has over 160 members including publishing companies, newspapers and magazines, TV, radio and pure online media. Its census for 2007 makes interesting reading. Apparently, UK digital publishers experienced an average 60% increase in turnover in 2006, and are predicting an average of 72% growth for 2007 – double what they were forecasting from the year before. Total turnover for AOP members' digital operations increased to £575m, up from £344m the previous year. AOP members employ nearly

8,000 individuals in the digital side of their businesses, with 540 new jobs created in the last year alone by AOP members.

Publishers see broadband, mobile (and wireless) and communities as the biggest opportunities for the industry in 2007. Simon Waldman, AOP chairman and group director of digital strategy, Guardian Media Group, said: 'This is a remarkable set of figures. 2006 was a year of spectacular digital growth, innovation and investment by the UK's media industry – and our forecasts show there is no sign of this letting up' (www.ukaop.org.uk).

So, where the revolution is really happening is on the web, where sites such as YouTube and MySpace are changing the way people exchange information and interact with each other. YouTube rolled out another nine local sites in 2007 (the UK, Ireland, France, Italy, Netherlands, Spain, Poland, Brazil and Japan) and the phenomena shows no signs of slowing down. Although some people in the traditional media (especially journalists) see all this activity on the internet as a threat to their livelihoods, in fact, they should be seeing it as the most fantastic opportunity and should embrace it because this expansion will mean more work opportunities rather than less. As camera assistant Mark Sayers says: 'People should look towards the internet and new media for work because this is going to be one of the big growth areas.'

The 'next wave', aka 'ambient intelligence' or 'pervasive', 'transparent' or 'ubiquitous' computing will make up the domestic, consumer and business computing and communications environment of the future.

New media now forms a part of every sector from blue chip companies to games developers, broadcasters and publishers. The new media sector include jobs for technical and creative people involved in everything from programming to project management, software development and sales and marketing. According to a new trends report (*Overview of Anticipated Trends in the Future Use of Skills in the Audiovisual Industry to 2010*, 2004) by Skillset, looking at the future of industry until 2010, new media will also change some existing jobs. Skillset states:

'There is little available evidence to suggest that old skills will be discarded, entirely new skills required or new occupations created or dissolved within the next six years. This is in contrast to the video games and the interactive media industries in the 1990s where whole new industries were created. Rather there will be changes of emphasis in the skill sets required for certain key occupations. Craft-based or technical occupations, eg, camera, sound, lighting, editing, are set to change the least. The major changes in those areas have, in effect, already happened – principally the paradigmatic shift in switching to digital for shooting, editing and post-production in film and TV, and the establishment of online and mobile technologies and platforms.

'The biggest skill changes anticipated over the period to 2010 are, instead, within the higher level occupations associated with business and creative strategy. This covers a range of occupations concerned with planning, funding, co-ordinating, versioning, aggregating, packaging and selling audiovisual products and services. These include the roles of: producer, business development manager, managing director, market/audience analyst, scheduler and commissioning editor. It is anticipated that significant changes in emphasis within these roles will be required for the UK industry to fully develop and thrive over the next six years.'

Other jobs in new media include:

- **Web designer** – works to a brief to create the look of the pages of an internet site. Using programming techniques and internet tools, the web designer works on the 'back end' systems to ensure the site works properly, and on the 'front end' to ensure it looks good and is easy to navigate. The web designer converts his or her ideas to the web via design software and code including HTML (hypertext mark-up language). Making changes in response to feedback from a client is an important part of a web designer's job.

- **Multimedia programmer** – writes the programmes that create multimedia products. These are designed to work on many 'platforms' including interactive TV, CD-ROMs, DVDs, computer games and WAP phones. This is a technical and creative role.

- **Software engineer** (aka software developer or computer programmer) – designs software systems in response to a brief. The software engineer is responsible for maintaining and testing the software systems. Using programming applications and authoring tools, software engineers integrate text, video and sound. A software engineer may be supported by a coder.

CASH

Starting salaries are:

- **Internet/web professional** – somewhere in the region of £17,500, going up to £40,000 and above as career progresses[3]

- **Multimedia programmer** – around £18,000 to £35,000, going up to £50,000 plus when established[4]

- **Software engineer** – between £19,500 and £35,000, increasing to a high of around £80,000 when established.[4]

TOP TIP

Go to www.e-skills.com and www.prospects.ac.uk for more information on jobs and the IT industry. The *Media Guardian* (in both print and internet form) now includes New Media in its Creative and Media section (www.guardian.co.uk/jobs).

REAL LIVES – THE WEB DESIGNER

Andrew Clarke, 25, South African born, now based in Newcastle

The job
I work freelance, which really suits me. At the moment I'm working on a new website aimed at teenagers. My brief is to come up with a cutting-edge look and feel. It's fun because I can go quite mad with the design.

3. Figures from Connexions (www.connexions-direct.com)
4. Figures from Prospects (www.prospects.ac.uk)

Best bit

It's creative and satisfying when you see your final work go live. It's sociable. I'm always working with new teams of people on each job.

Worst bit

Clients don't always know what they want. So even when you have followed their brief they might want to change something fundamental to the design so you've got to basically start again. Also timings can be a problem. I'm always up against deadlines and I find deadlines a bit challenging! But I'm a perfectionist, so even if I do deliver a bit late the client is always really happy with the result.

TOP TIP

For some creative ideas read *Creative Magazine* at www.creativemag.com.

JARGON BUSTER

Java – not coffee, but a programming language used on the internet.

REAL LIVES – THE NEW MEDIA EDITOR

Cait O'Riordan, Assistant Editor, BBC News On Demand

The job

I edit the output for broadband news and interactive television news. It's red-button stuff.

Best bit

I enjoy dealing with breaking news and I like the fact the job keeps changing as new ways of presenting news are developed in response to new technology.

Worst bit
That's got to be getting up at five in the morning on early starts or finishing late on late starts. The shifts are ten hours but I only work four days a week so that's a good thing.

CAREER LADDER

Assistant editor, BBC News On Demand
↑
Senior broadcast journalist, BBC News On Demand
↑
Broadcast journalist, BBC News On Demand
↑
Internet news writer, ITN
↑
TV documentary producer
↑
National radio news
↑
Local radio news
↑
University degree

TOP TIP

Go to www.bbc.co.uk to find out more about interactive television news.

REAL LIVES – THE SENIOR WEB DEVELOPER

Leo Lapworth, 28, from London, works for Foxton's Estate Agents. Foxton's site has won the British Interactive Media Association's Grand Prix Award and Public Services Award.

How many visitors do you get?
Monthly we get over 4 million page impressions.

How many are there in your team?
Three.

How did you get your job?
I was head hunted from my CV on the net.

Best bit
I have never been bothered about the type of website I work on, it is the functionality and people that make it enjoyable. Foxton's aims to be the best London property website there is and I think the award proves we achieve that. The exciting thing is we are continuously trying to make it better. The web team also works on many of the internal systems at Foxton's, which allows us to meet different types of challenge. The web has been the most significant development for estate agents over the last few years and I see it continuing to make a big impact as we continue to explore other avenues such as SMS, email and any other avenues available.

Worst bit
There's never enough time to do everything you would like to, but I'd rather that than be bored!

Flexibility
The great thing about working in new media is that once you've got your skills you can work in most sectors.

JARGON BUSTER

Front end and *back end* – yes, it does sound weird. But it's really quite simple. The front end on an internet site is what the user sees and the back end is the technical stuff that makes it happen.

REAL LIVES – THE MANAGING DIRECTOR OF A NEW MEDIA HEALTH CONSULTANCY

The job
I manage Health Technology Solutions Ltd, act as a consultant, account manager, project manager and – due to experience – occasional hands-on web development. Work focuses primarily on the health sector/NHS.

Best bit
The satisfaction of providing solutions to client problems and delivering solutions.

Worst bit
There isn't one!

Career path
I began as an IT support officer in the NHS and progressed up into IT management. I took on the role of project manager/director for national web-based project management (initially by taking a chance and personally setting up a website providing information on the NHS and being asked to join the national team and do it for them instead). Then I left to join a private sector company as an IT director producing websites for pharmaceutical companies in health promotion. After seeing the company through floatation, I left to set up Health Technology Solutions Ltd as an internet/web consultancy and development supplier for health sector/NHS organisations and projects.

TOP TIP

If gaming's your thing, go to the Independent Games Developers' Trade Association – www.tiga.org – to find out more.

RELATED OCCUPATIONS

- Applications developer

- Information technology consultant

- New business development

- Systems analyst

- Systems designer

- Technical author.

CHAPTER 9

Getting in and getting on

JOB HUNTING

Getting your first job in the media can be the most difficult part. First decide what it is you want to do by researching properly. Once you are focused on which area of the media you would like to work in, it will make it easier to land your perfect first job.

Look in the specialist press for advertised jobs (see below for details for each sector), check out the internet and read Monday's *Guardian* for their weekly media jobs section. Also ask everyone and anyone you know who might be able to help you get some work experience. You will need to be resourceful. Don't be embarrassed to ask your parents' friends or your friend's parents' friends or your parents' parents' friends! Leave no stone unturned. They will understand – everybody had to start somewhere! Go to www.work-experience.org for more information on work experience.

TRAINING

Even if you are a graduate, vocational training may be useful to give you the edge over other candidates (see below for contact details for each sector). It's a good idea to do some work experience first so that you can decide whether you will enjoy working in your chosen area. If you can't afford to pay for training, don't despair. In a lot of media jobs you can learn on the job. You just need to be able to throw yourself in at the deep end.

INTERNSHIP AND GRADUATE TRAINEESHIPS

Some of the larger broadcasters, newspapers and publishing houses offer limited places on their graduate trainee programmes. These offer excellent training and possibilities for career advancement. While doing your research, find out what large organisations like the BBC and Penguin can offer you. It is difficult to get on to a training scheme, but most organisations provide a detailed description of what they are looking for on their websites. Find out about these as early as possible so that you can apply in time and also fill in any gaps.

NETWORKING

Getting your foot in the door and then progressing up the media career ladder will depend on your networking skills. Because so many media jobs require long hours in stressful conditions, being a 'people person' is an important part of many jobs. If you make friends on every job you work on, you will have a network of colleagues to tell you about new job opportunities. Word of mouth is a powerful tool in the media. We've done some networking for you! Scouring the country to find those in the know, we've asked for advice from them so you can get ahead and get on. Read on for their gems of wisdom!

YOUR CV

People who break into media are likely to do so by sending in a CV and covering letter to a specific person in an organisation than by answering a job advertisement. Skillset did a survey of freelancers working in the audio-visual industries and discovered that between one-fifth and a half of those starting out got their first job by contacting their employer rather than answering an ad.

However, a lot of CVs just go 'on file' – put in a drawer somewhere never to see the light of day again. It will help if you target where you are sending your CV.

- Think about where you are sending your CV. Research companies with products you love. If you love a particular book, find out who published it (easy these days with the help of the mighty Amazon, go to www.amazon.co.uk); if you love a television programme, find out who made it.

- Do some research in the specialist press to find out what is being made now (see details below). Inside knowledge goes a long way. It makes you look professional and focused and you can match your skills to a particular project.

It also helps if your CV looks good and is word perfect. CHECK AND DOUBLE-CHECK YOUR CV FOR MISTAKES. Finding mistakes in a CV drives employers mad and makes you look sloppy. Most entry-level jobs will require administration in some form, for which attention to detail will be important. Spelling mistakes give the impression that you are not good at detail and that possibly you haven't put much effort in.

Find out the name of the correct person to send your CV to. Otherwise you will look lazy. And spell it right. Ever got junk mail through the post that spells your name wrong or gets your gender wrong? Well that's the kind of impression you want to avoid.

TOP TIP

www.skillset.org can help you create the perfect CV, as can Channel 4's *Brilliant Careers* website at www.channel4.com/4talent.

INTERVIEW TIPS

Most of how to behave in an interview is common sense and you've probably been through it before – but just to refresh your memory:

- Never go unprepared to an interview. Always research the output of any company you are going to see. If you turn up at a publisher and don't know what books they publish, they will think you aren't interested. If you manage to secure an interview with a TV company and haven't watched any of their programmes they'll wonder why you turned up! Don't blow precious chances – do your research before the interview.

- People in the media are passionate about what they do. You will need to convince them that you are passionate about their area too. Have a few ideas up your sleeve so you can impress an interviewer with your creativity. Remember, in many sectors the 16–34 market is key because advertisers chase that age group. There's big money in TV series that have high ratings in that age group, for example. As a younger person your ideas will be taken seriously. Go to www.channel4.com/4talent for some inspiration.

- Shake hands with the interviewer when you walk into the room. Stand up straight. And when you leave, shake hands again and thank them for their time.

- Smile, and try to convey what the interview is – a fantastic opportunity for you to break into the industry of your dreams.

- Carefully choose what to wear. Inside information helps, so ask someone who works in the industry if you can. You don't always need to wear a suit but you do always need to wear clean clothes!

- Keep your hands in your lap if you're feeling nervous. You will look less nervous if your hands are still.

- Look people straight in the eye.

- It's not essential, but a letter written to the interviewer to say how much you enjoyed meeting him or her comes across as courteous.

TV AND FILM

In 2003, a comprehensive training strategy was launched by the UK Film Council and Skillset that set up a number of new film training initiatives. The Skillset Screen Academy Network is a UK-wide group of centres of excellence in film education and training. They offer the highest quality of skills training and their aim is to ensure the UK has the most talented and skilled workforce in the world, both now and in the future.

The Network is made up of six Skillset screen academies: Bournemouth Screen Academy, Screen Academy Wales, Screen Academy Scotland, the London College of Communication (LCC), Ealing Institute of Media (EIM), and the National Film and TV School (for more information on each go to www.skillset.org).

Also, the world's first international centre dedicated to the business of film, the Film Business Academy, has been set up at the Cass Business School in London offering the UK's first ever MBA in film (see www.filmbusinessacademy.com).

Here's some advice from those who know on routes into the industry:

'Exhaust any contacts you might have, ask everyone if they know anyone who works in TV. Unfortunately I didn't know anyone, but I got my runner's job from an ad in the *Guardian* – it was luck. Blag it the whole way too! I started filming on a shoot and I'd never done it before. Be confident, but also be a little bit humble and nice to people. It's about skill and vision and creativity but ultimately it's about people. There are always 20 other people who could do your job.'

Freelance kids' TV director

'If you want to become a broadcast journalist, do one of the specific broadcast journalism courses. I did mine after I graduated with a degree in French. The best piece of advice I ever got was to start out in independent local radio. They've got so much less money than somewhere like the BBC so you are very quickly given a lot of responsibility as it's all hands on deck. You will be paid appallingly but it will stand you in good stead for the future. It's incredibly hard work and probably will include night-time shifts, but you've just got to bite the bullet for about a year and a half. You'll learn more than you imagined possible.'

TV news reporter

'I got my running job through a friend. I put the word out that I was looking for a running job. He's now moved on to a job as an editing assistant. To be a runner you've just got to keep focused on what you want out of it. You certainly don't need brains to do running, just staying power!'

Post-production runner for TV and video

'When I was working as a production assistant on the *Today* programme John Humphrys gave me the best piece of advice of my career. He told me to go to local radio and get my experience there. He was right – you get amazing experience and you can make mistakes and learn from them in front of a smaller audience.'

TV news presenter

BECOMING A PRESENTER
To become a TV presenter you need to make a **showreel**. There's some really useful information about how to put one together on the Channel 4 website: www.channel4.com/4careers.

They say you need to:

● grab the viewer's attention in the first minute

● make it fun and interesting

● keep it short – four to five minutes

● include a mix of short scenes (perhaps a live outside report and a mock interview)

● do it on the cheap – ask family and friends

● when sending out your showreel always send a copy, not your original – you're unlikely to get it back!

'Without a doubt television is one of the most fun jobs you can have. But if you want financial security you should go into the management side of the business.

'As programmes are made with smaller and smaller budgets, these days technical skills are becoming increasingly important. Being able to work a camera, do the sound and editing are all useful skills nowadays, even for a producer. To become a producer, I would advise that you try and get a running or administrative job with a big company like Granada or the BBC and be trained in-house. Independents have to throw you out once your contract is up because they can't afford to keep you on. Everyone's salary has to come out of a programme budget. If you do want to work for an independent, try a larger company that has a high turnover of popular programmes and is likely to have more money to be able to keep you on for a bit. It's easy to work out which the successful companies are. Just watch TV! The name of the production company that made a programme will always be displayed in the credits at the end. Most production companies have their own websites with contact details.'

Freelance TV producer

'Do what I did and start out getting some work experience. When you do land a job as a production assistant, don't expect to be making films immediately! Although a production assistant's job can be exciting, it's a secretarial role – very few boys do it because of that. But in the end most producers are men.'

Film production assistant

'Write to a casting director and volunteer to work for free. It's good to get DV skills as you are likely to have to film auditions.'

Film assistant casting director

'Join the BBC. You get good training and lots of money. Phone around all the production companies to start you on your career path. Either get a runner's position or find an assistant/secretarial role in a development team.'

Script editor

SPECIALIST PRESS

Ariel (in-house BBC magazine – call 01709 768165)
AV – Audio Visual Magazine (www.avmag.co.uk)
Broadcast (www.broadcastnow.co.uk)
Campaign (www.brandrepublic.com)
Media Guardian (www.media.guardian.co.uk)
Media Week (www.mediaweek.co.uk)
Press Gazette (www.pressgazette.co.uk)
Screen International (www.screendaily.com)
Televisual (www.televisual.com)
The Stage (www.thestage.co.uk)

WEBSITES

www.4rfv.co.uk
www.bbc.co.uk
www.channel4.com/4careers
www.filmcast.org
www.film-tv.co.uk
www.guardian.co.uk
www.monster.com
www.productionbase.co.uk
www.shootingpeople.org
www.startintv.com
www.ukscreen.com

COURSE INFORMATION

British Film Institute (www.bfi.org.uk/education/talkscourses)
Learn Direct (www.learndirect.co.uk)
Skillset (www.skillset.org/careers)

RADIO

Some words of advice:

'You do need to be the right kind of person to present. You've got to be talkative and able to interact with your listeners. If you are the right kind of personality, then it's possible to make it. You need to have passion because you have to be able to get up the same energy time and again and you've got to put yourself a bit out there. Community radio is a great place to start. While you're working you can get a demo – it will help you make your next career move.'

Community radio DJ

'A postgraduate broadcasting course with an emphasis on practical skills is useful. Work experience is essential. I started a magazine at university and that helped me get on the course and my first job.'

Researcher on radio documentaries

SPECIALIST PRESS
Ariel (in-house BBC magazine – call 01709 768165)
Broadcast (www.broadcastnow.co.uk)
Media Guardian (www.media.guardian.co.uk)

WEBSITES
www.bbc.co.uk
www.channel4.com
www.guardian.co.uk
www.hospitalradio.co.uk
www.mediauk.com
www.radio-now.co.uk
www.ukradio.com

COURSE INFORMATION
Broadcast Journalism Training Council (www.bjtc.org.uk)
Radio Centre (www.radiocentre.org)
Radio Academy (www.radioacademy.org)

NEWSPAPERS AND MAGAZINES

Some tips on getting on in newspapers and magazines.

'I would say definitely do a journalism course. I did one after university. I'm glad I chose this route as my degree in politics and sociology was fascinating and I learnt excellent writing and researching skills whilst doing my degree. These are useful skills for news reporting. What I regret is not doing more research before I chose my postgraduate journalism course. Some courses prepare you more for national newspapers and have links with those and others prepare you more for local newspapers. I didn't realise this when I found my course. Always ask what aspect of journalism your course is geared towards, then you can go in with your eyes open. Also, find out where ex-graduates have got placements. For example, I know people often get good placements after the Cardiff course – Cardiff School of Journalism, Media and Cultural Studies, www.cf.ac.uk/jomec/ – as it's considered one of the best places to do a postgrad journalism course. After all, it's likely you will have to pay for the course yourself, so make sure you get value for money and ensure whatever course you choose is approved by the National Council for the Training of Journalists (NCTJ), www.nctj.com/.'

Senior reporter, local newspaper

'Do work experience in a magazine or newspaper office. The key is to try to make yourself noticed without being obnoxious. Most bottom-rung jobs in magazines don't require a huge amount of talent: you're most likely to be taken on if you come across as likeable, smiley and efficient. These days, people spend a vast amount of their lives at work, so when they take on junior staff, they are looking for people who'll be nice to have around and who'll get the job done with minimum fuss.'

Magazine editor

'There isn't a traditional career path for a picture editor. Interest in photography and images is essential and a lot of picture editors come from a photographic background. You don't have to be particularly academic. I've got a degree but it's not in any way a necessity for the job. If you want to work for a newspaper, choose carefully, as some papers place a lot more emphasis on images than others. For example, in my opinion, the *Guardian* or the *Independent* use more exciting images than most other national papers. Make sure you look at how different papers use images and try to work for the one that appeals to you most. Getting work experience on a picture desk is a good way to find out if the job is for you. You will be taken more seriously if you can display a real interest and love of pictures and photography. Securing a work experience position isn't easy. Try using any contact you can – ask everyone you know in case they know anyone who works on a local paper, magazine or even a national. Failing that, be really persistent. You might just catch someone on the right day.'

Picture editor, national newspaper

'I didn't do a journalism course. But a lot of journalists find them useful. I think the key is to start writing as early as possible. Find opportunities to write at school and university. Start freelancing as soon as you can, send off ideas to editors and make as many contacts as possible. A local newspaper is an excellent place to start after university.'

International news agency reporter

SPECIALIST PRESS
Ariel (in-house BBC magazine – call 01709 364 721)
Media Guardian (www.media.guardian.co.uk)
Press Gazette (www.pressgazette.co.uk)

ORGANISATIONS AND WEBSITES
BBC (www.bbc.co.uk)
National Union of Journalists (www.nuj.org.uk)

COURSE INFORMATION
National Council for the Training of Journalists (NCTJ) (www.nctj.com)
Newspaper Society (www.newspapersoc.org.uk)

BOOKS AND JOURNALS

Some words of wisdom:

'Do get some design and production training. For example, to become a book designer you will need to be trained in typography and layout. Once trained, look for job advertisements in the specialised press or approach a publishing recruitment agency to see if they can find you an entry-level position like a production assistant. Other routes in include work experience.'

Assistant editor, book publishing

'I'd advise doing a relevant postgraduate course that creates some sort of basic understanding of the industry and then join a publishing recruitment agency. Work experience is useful if you've got nothing else happening. In my experience, however, publishers tend to have a lot of people doing work experience at any one time with little hope of a job at the end. You are more likely to secure a position through the course/recruitment agency route.'

Head of production, book publishing

'For specialist roles in production and design some relevant qualification is very helpful, but getting work experience and temporary work in trade publishing shows enthusiasm and commitment.'

Production manager, book publishing

'You've got to make your own career in publishing. You need to be really keen and make your own opportunities. I'll never forget a friend of mine who started at Routledge at the same time as me. She went to every department asking them what they did and finding out what the opportunities were for her. You have to be as enthusiastic and self-motivated as that to get on.

'Other routes to get into publishing include the traditional secretarial route, though I would advise going for editorial/marketing/production assistant-type jobs if you don't want to get sidelined into becoming a PA. Working in bookselling will also give you a fabulously commercial insight into what sells, and what stays resolutely on the shelves, and I can recommend that as another route in – though be warned, this is more likely to get you into the marketing side, than the editorial side.

'I would also suggest that if you are at college, get a job selling books in your holidays, do some temping for a publishing company or anything at all connected with publishing, which shows you are willing and able. I would also recommend that you do as my friend did, and try and understand all the processes involved in publishing a book – when it works it is a cohesive process, which demands good communication and understanding of your colleagues' problems. If you can do that, then you will go far!'

Commissioning editor, book publishing

SPECIALIST PRESS
The Bookseller (www.thebookseller.com)
Print Week (www.printweek.com)
Publishing News (www.publishingnews.co.uk)

ORGANISATIONS AND WEBSITES
Association of On-Line Publishers (AOP) (www.ukaop.org.uk)
Book Careers (www.bookcareers.com)

Booksellers' Association of the United Kingdom and Ireland Ltd
(BA) (www.booksellers.org.uk)
Publishers Association (PA) (www.publishers.org.uk)

COURSES
Publishers Association (www.publishers.org.uk)
Publishing Training Centre (www.train4publishing.co.uk)

Go to www.thebookseller.co.uk to find out more about publishing
recruitment agencies.

NEW MEDIA

Advice from people working in new media:

'I come from an art background and I taught myself all the back
end stuff. I would say do a course if you want to, but the key is to
start designing. Do websites for your friends and let people know
what you're doing. If you're good, word will soon get around. But
market yourself too. Once you've done a few sites, get business
cards, set up your own website and start pitching for business.'
Web designer

'Work in local papers or local radio or in online news for local TV.
Do at least two years in local news. For a job at BBC Online that
news experience will give you a good head start.'
Assistant editor, BBC News On Demand

SPECIALIST PRESS
Creative Review (www.creativereview.co.uk)
New Media Age (www.nma.co.uk)
Revolution (www.brandrepublic.com)

ORGANISATIONS AND WEBSITES
British Computer Society (BCS) (www.bcs.org.uk)
British Interactive Multimedia Association (BIMA)
 (www.bima.co.uk)
Institution of Analysts and Programmers (IAP) (www.iap.org.uk)
Institute for the Management of Information Systems (IMIS)
 (www.imis.org.uk)

COURSE INFORMATION

British Film Institute (BFI) (www.bfi.org.uk)
Independent Games Developers' Trade Association (www.tiga.org)
Skillset (Sector Skills Council for the Audio Visual Industries)
(www.skillset.org)

CHAPTER 10

Further information

If you're interested in any of the careers in this book, now's the time to start researching further. If you can't find the right information, ask. With loads of interactive services available like LearnDirect it is always possible to email a specialist for some specific careers advice. Go to www.learndirect.co.uk for more information.

GENERAL

Benn's Media Directory, Hollis Publishing Ltd
Guardian, Guardian Newspapers Ltd (www.guardian.co.uk), daily
Guardian Media Directory, Guardian Books, annual
Press Gazette, Wilmington Media, weekly
Willings Press Guide, Cision, annual

TV AND FILM

BFI – British Film Institute
21 Stephen Street
London W1T 1LN
Tel: 020 7255 1444
Website: www.bfi.org.uk

BKSTS – The Moving Image Society
Pinewood Studios, Pinewood Road
Iver Heath
Buckinghamshire SLO 0NH
Tel: 01753 656656
Website: www.bksts.com

British Academy of Film and Television Arts (BAFTA)
195 Piccadilly
London W1J 9LN
Tel: 020 7734 0022
Website: www.bafta.org

FT2
3rd Floor
18–20 Southwark Street
London SE1 1TJ
Tel: 020 7407 0344
Website: www.ft2.org.uk

Office of Communications (OFCOM)
Riverside House
2a Southwark Bridge Road
Southwark
London SE1 9HA
Tel: 020 7981 3000
Website: www.ofcom.org.uk

Producers' Alliance for Cinema and Television (PACT)
Proctor House
1 Proctor Street
Holborn
London WC1 6DW
Tel: 020 7067 4367
Website: www.pact.co.uk

Royal Television Society
5th Floor
Kildare House
3 Dorset Rise
London EC4Y 8EN
Tel: 020 7822 2810
Website: www.rts.org.uk

Skillset
Prospect House
80–110 New Oxford Street
London WC1A 1HB
Tel: 020 7520 5757
Website: www.skillset.org

UNIONS, GUILDS AND TRADE ASSOCIATIONS

Advertising Producers' Association
47 Beak Street
London W1F 9SE
Tel: 020 7434 2651
Website: www.a-p-a.net

Broadcasting, Entertainment, Cinematograph and Theatre Union (BECTU)
373–377 Clapham Road
London SW9 9BT
Tel: 020 7346 0900
Website: www.bectu.org.uk

Broadcast Journalism Training Council
18 Miller's Close
Rippingale, near Bourne
Lincolnshire PE10 0TH
Tel: 01778 440025
Website: www.bjtc.org.uk

Casting Directors' Guild
PO Box 34403
London W6 0YG
Tel: 020 8741 1951
Website: www.thecdg.co.uk

Directors' Guild of Great Britain
4 Windmill Street
London W1T 2HZ
Tel: 020 7580 9131
Website: www.dggb.co.uk

The Film Business Academy
CASS Business School
106 Bunhill Row
London EC1Y 8TZ
Tel: 020 7040 8600
Website: www.cass.city.ac.uk

First Light Movies
Unit 6, Third Floor
The Bond
180–182 Fazeley Street
Birmingham B5 5SE
Tel: 0121 753 4866
Website: www.firstlightmovies.com

Futureshorts
34–35 Berwick Street
London W1F 8RP
Tel: 020 7734 3883
Website: www.futureshorts.com

Guild of British Camera Technicians
GBCT, c/o Panavision UK
Metropolitan Centre
Bristol Road
Greenford
Middlesex UB6 8GD
Tel: 020 8813 1999
Website: www.gbct.org

Guild of Location Managers
c/o Film London
Suite 6.10
The Tea Building
56 Shoreditch Street
London E1 6JJ
Tel: 020 7387 8787
Website: www.golm.org.uk

Guild of TV Cameramen
1 Churchill Road

Whitchurch
Tavistock
Devon PL19 9B
Tel: 01822 614405
Website: www.gtc.org.uk

Guild of Vision Mixers
85 Oliphant Street
London W10 4EE
Website: www.guildofvisionmixers.co.uk

Institute of Broadcast Sound
PO Box 932
Guildford GU4 7WW
Tel: 01483 575450
Website: www.ibs.org.uk

The John Brabourne Awards
c/o The Cinema and Television Benevolent Fund
22 Golden Square
London W1F 9AD
Website: www.ctbf.co.uk

MEDIABOX
Website: www.media-box.co.uk

Music Video Producers Association
26 Noel Street
London W1V 3RD
Tel: 020 7434 2651
Website: www.mvpa.co.uk

National Union of Journalists (NUJ)
Headland House
308–312 Gray's Inn Road
London WC1X 8DP
Tel: 020 7278 7916
Website: www.nuj.org.uk

Production Guild of Great Britain
Pinewood Studios
Pinewood Road

Iver Heath
Buckinghamshire SLO ONH
Tel: 01753 651767
Website: www.productionguild.com

Production Managers' Association
Ealing Studios
Ealing Green
London W5 5EP
Tel: 020 8758 8699
Website: www.pma.org.uk

Professional Lighting and Sound Association
Redoubt House
1 Edward Road
Eastbourne BN23 8AS
Tel: 01323 524120
Website: www.plasa.org

Society of Television Lighting Directors
Website: www.stld.org.uk

Teledwyr Annibynnool Cymru (TAC)
33–35 West Bute Street
Cardiff CF10 5LH
Tel: 02920 463322
Website: www.teledwyr.com

Unite the Union
Membership and Administration
Hayes Court
West Common Road
Hayes BR2 7AU
Tel: 0845 850 4242
Website: www.amicustheunion.org

Women in Film and Television
2 Wedgwood Mews
12–13 Greek Street
London W1D 4BB
Tel: 020 7287 1701
Website: www.wftv.org.uk

Writers' Guild of Great Britain
15 Britannia Street
London WC1X 9JN
Tel: 020 7833 0777
Website: www.writersguild.org.uk

RADIO

Broadcast Journalism Training Council
18 Miller's Close
Rippingale, near Bourne
Lincolnshire PE10 0TH
Tel: 01778 440 025
Website: www.bjtc.org.uk

Radio Centre
77 Shaftesbury Avenue
London W1D 5DU
Tel: 020 7306 2603
Website: www.radiocentre.org

Community Media Association
The Workstation
15 Paternoster Row
Sheffield S1 2BX
Tel: 0114 279 5219
Website: www.commedia.org.uk

NEWSPAPER AND MAGAZINES

Daily Mail and General Trust plc
Head and Registered Office
Northcliffe House
2 Derry Street
London W8 5TT
Tel: 020 7938 6000
Website: www.dmgt.co.uk

EMAP
40 Bernard Street
London WC1N 1LW
Tel: 020 7278 1452
Website: www.emap.com

Guardian Media Group plc
60 Farringdon Road
London EC1R 3GA
Tel: 020 7278 2332
Website: www.gmgplc.co.uk

Haymarket Publishing Ltd
174 Hammersmith Road
London W6 7JP
Tel: 020 8267 5000
Website: www.haymarketgroup.co.uk

IPC Magazines
The Blue Fin Building
110 Southwark Street
London SE1 0SU
Tel: 020 3148 5000
Website: www.ipcmedia.com

National Council for the Training of Journalists (NCTJ)
New Granary
Station Road
Newport
Saffron Walden
Essex CB11 3BL
Tel: 01799 544014
Website: www.nctj.com

National Union of Journalists (NUJ)
Headland House
308–312 Gray's Inn Road
London WC1X 8DP
Tel: 020 7278 7916
Website: www.nuj.org.uk

The National Magazine Company Ltd
National Magazine House
72 Broadwick Street
London W1F 9EP
Tel: 020 7439 5000
Website: www.natmags.co.uk

Newspaper Society
St. Andrew's House
18–20 St. Andrew Street
London EC4A 3AY
Tel: 020 7632 7400
Website: www.newspapersoc.org.uk

Newsquest
Unecol House
819 London Road
North Cheam
Surrey SM3 9BN
Tel: 020 8329 9244
Website: www.newsquest.co.uk

Periodical Publishers Association Ltd (PPA)
Queens House
28 Kingsway
London WC2B 6JR
Tel: 020 7404 4166
Website: www.ppa.co.uk

Picture Research Association
1 Willow Court
London EC2A 4QB
Website: www.picture-research.org.uk

Press Association
292 Vauxhall Bridge Road
London SW1V 1AE
Tel: 0870 120 3200
Website: www.thepagroup.com

Trinity Mirror plc
One Canada Square
Canary Wharf
London E14 5AP
Tel: 020 7293 3000
Website: www.trinitymirror.com

BOOKS AND JOURNALS

Association of Learned and Professional Society Publishers
Blenheim House
120 Church Street
Brighton BN1 1AU
Website: www.alpsp.org.uk

Association of On-Line Publishers (AOP)
Queens House
28 Kingsway
London WC2B 6JR
Tel: 020 7404 4166
Website: www.ukaop.org.uk

Blackwell Publishing Ltd
9600 Garsington Road
Oxford OX4 2DQ
Tel: 01865 776868
Website: www.blackwellpublishing.com

Bloomsbury Publishing Plc
36 Soho Square
London W1D 3QY
Tel: 020 7494 2111
Website: www.bloomsbury.com

Booksellers Association of the United Kingdom and Ireland Ltd (BA)
Minster House
272 Vauxhall Bridge Road
London SW1V 1BA
Tel: 020 7802 0802
Website: www.booksellers.org.uk

Cambridge University Press
The Edinburgh Building
Shaftesbury Road
Cambridge CB2 8RU
Tel: 01223 312393
Website: www.cambridge.org

Hachette Livre UK
338 Euston Road
London NW1 3BH
Tel: 020 7873 6000
Website: www.hodderheadline.co.uk

HarperCollins
77–85 Fulham Palace Road
London W6 8JB
Tel: 020 8741 7070
Website: www.harpercollins.co.uk

The Irish Book Publishers Association
25 Denzille Lane
Dublin 2
Tel: +353 1 639 4868
Website: www.publishingireland.com

London College of Communication
Elephant & Castle
London SE1 6SB
Tel: 020 7514 6569
Website: www.lcc.arts.ac.uk

Macmillan Publishers Ltd
4 Crinan Street
London N1 9XW
Tel: 020 7833 4000
Website: www.macmillan.com

Music Publishers Association Ltd
6th Floor, British Music House
26 Berners Street
London W1T 3LR
Tel: 020 7580 0126
Website: www.mpaonline.org.uk

Oxford University Press
Great Clarendon Street
Oxford OX2 6DP
Tel: 01865 556 767
Website: www.oup.co.uk

Pearson
80 Strand
London WC2R 0RL
Tel: 020 7010 2000
Website: www.pearson.com

Pearson Education
Edinburgh Gate
Harlow
Essex CM20 2JE
Tel: 01279 623623
Website: www.pearsoned.co.uk

Penguin Books Ltd
80 Strand
London WC2R 0RL
Tel: 020 7010 3000
Website: www.penguin.co.uk

Publishers Association (PA)
29b Montague Street
London WC1B 5BW
Tel: 020 7691 9191
Website: www.publishers.org.uk

Publishing Scotland
Scottish Book Centre
137 Dundee Street
Edinburgh EH11 1BG
Tel: 0131 228 6866
Website: www.publishingscotland.org

Publishing Training Centre
45 East Hill
Wandsworth

London SW18 2QZ
Tel: 020 8874 2718
Website: www.train4publishing.co.uk

Reed Business Information
Quadrant House
The Quadrant
Sutton
Surrey SM2 5AS
Tel: 020 8652 3500
Website: www.reedbusiness.co.uk

Reed Elsevier
1–3 Strand
London WC2N 5JR
Tel: 020 7930 7077
Website: www.reed-elsevier.com

Society for Editors and Proofreaders (SfEP)
Riverbank House
1 Putney Bridge Approach
London SW6 3JD
Tel: 020 7736 3278
Website: www.sfep.org.uk

Society of Young Publishers
Endeavour House
189 Shaftesbury Avenue
London WC2H 3TJ
Website: www.thesyp.org.uk

T&F Informa plc
2 Park Square
Milton Park
Abingdon MP14 4RN
Tel: 020 7017 6000
Website: www.taylorandfrancisgroup.com

Random House
20 Vauxhall Bridge Road
London SW1V 2SA
Tel: 020 7840 8400
Website: www.randomhouse.co.uk

NEW MEDIA

British Computer Society
First Floor, Block D
North Star House
North Star Avenue
Swindon SW2 1FA
Tel: 0845 300 4417
www.bcs.org.uk

British Interactive Multimedia Association
Briarlea House
Southend Road
Billericay CM11 2B7
Tel: 012776 58107
www.bima.co.uk

e-skills UK
1 Castle Lane
London SW1E 6DR
Tel: 0207 963 8920
www.e-skills.com

Independent Games Developers' Trade Association
Brighton Business Centre
95 Ditchling Road
Brighton BN1 4ST
Tel: 0845 0941 1095
www.tiga.org

Institute of Analysts and Programmers
Charles House
36 Culmington Road
London W13 9NH
Tel: 020 8567 2118
www.iap-online.org.uk

International Games Developers Association
19 Mantua Road
Mt Royal

NJ 08061
USA
Tel: +1 856 423 2990
www.igda.org

National Computing Centre (NCC)
International Press Centre
15th Floor
76 Shoe Lane
London EC4A 3JB
Tel: 020 7842 7999
www.ncc.co.uk